CW01654628

Somatic Shamanism:

Your Fleshy Knowing as the Tree of Life

Kay Louise Aldred

Girl God Books

Cover Art by Kat Shaw

ISBN: 978-82-93725-39-8

Girl God Books are also available at discount for retail, wholesale, and bulk purchase. For details, contact us at support@girlgod.org.

www.thegirlgod.com

Girl God Books

Making Love with the Divine: Sacred, Ecstatic and Erotic Experiences

Making Love with the Divine starts the process of unravelling and undoing this insidious and false programming, showcasing and story-telling the *sacred, erotic, and ecstatic experiences* of today's 'ordinary' women, narrating and reflecting upon their accounts of day-to-day communion and union with the Divine. Inspired by their sharing, practises are offered in each section of the book for the reader to begin to forge their own unique and direct pathway of lovemaking with the Divine.

Mentorship with Goddess: Growing Sacred Womanhood

Mentorship with Goddess is a workbook – a year-long programme – a rite of passage – especially useful for the transition into autonomous adulthood – and also for the menopause journey. The programme can be undertaken solo or as a group. The specific aim is growing Sacred Womanhood. *Mentorship with Goddess* is an embodied education and evolution, which combines metacognition, intuition, and instinct. It is principally about discovering, accepting, and loving yourself, and simultaneously protecting and vulnerably showing up as your whole Self in the world.

Rainbow Goddess: Celebrating Neurodiversity

Rainbow Goddess lives within the full spectrum of the human mind. There is not one way of thinking, learning, or behaving that she does not inhabit fully and sanctify. This carnival and inclusive Goddess celebrates the gifts of those whose mind's exist and operate outside the box of society's 'norms' and she trumpets the creativity, visions and uniqueness of these humans. Rainbow Goddess also protectively arcs around them when they encounter the struggles of patriarchal expectation and judgement of being both neurodiverse and a woman. This Girl God Anthology showcases the voices and art of women as they express their experiences of neurodiversity.

The Crone Initiation: Women Speak on the Menopause Journey

The Crone Initiation is an Anthology of women's experiences of perimenopause and menopause, and the part Goddess plays in this journey. Crone's presence in the breakdowns and breakthroughs, the disintegration and rebuilding, is expressed through words and art. Meaning is reclaimed and the power of the Elder restored.

Re-Membering with Goddess: Healing the Patriarchal Perpetuation of Trauma

Re-Membering with Goddess is an anthology of women's experiences of trauma—trauma as a result of patriarchy; trauma perpetuated by patriarchy; and how through personal healing of trauma the Goddess is re-membered, re-embodied and resurrected.

As repeating loops of trauma restriction are released—in the mind, body and nervous system—Goddess is re-embodied and rises... and the patriarchy falls.

Just as I Am: Hymns Affirming the Divine Female

What is a Hermnal? It's the collective sigh of our ancestral Grandmothers. It's a means of drawing us closer together as Sisters. It is a compilation of songs that affirms our Sacredness, apart from Man, and assures us that we are Sovereign Beings and Creatrixes, too. And it is our Love Gift of Gratitude to Mama.

In Defiance of Oppression – The Legacy of Boudicca

An anthology that encapsulates the Spirit of the defiant warrior in a modern apathetic age. No longer will the voices of our sisters go unheard, as the ancient Goddesses return to the battlements, calling to ignite the spark within each and every one of us – to defy oppression wherever we find it, and stand together in solidarity.

Warrior Queen: Answering the Call of The Morrigan

A powerful anthology about the Irish Celtic Goddess. Each contributor brings The Morrigan to life with unique stories that invite readers to partake and inspire them to pen their own. Included are essays, poems, stories, chants, rituals, and art from dozens of story-tellers and artists from around the world, illustrating and recounting the many ways this powerful Goddess of war, death, and prophecy has changed their lives.

Re-visioning Medusa: From Monster to Divine Wisdom

A remarkable collection of essays, poems, and art by scholars who have researched Her, artists who have envisioned Her, and women who have known Her in their personal story. All have spoken with Her and share something of their communion in this anthology.

Inanna's Ascent: Reclaiming Female Power

Inanna's Ascent examines how females can rise from the underworld and reclaim their power, sovereignly expressed through poetry, prose and visual art. All contributors are extraordinary women in their own right, who have been through some difficult life lessons—and are brave enough to share their stories.

New Love: a reprogramming toolbox for undoing the knots

A powerful combination of emotional/spiritual techniques, art and inspiring words for women who wish to move away from patriarchal thought. *New Love* includes a mixture of compelling thoughts and suggestions for each day, along with a "toolbox" to help you change the parts of your life you want to heal.

*"The body remembers, the bones remember,
the joints remember, even the little finger remembers.
Memory is lodged in pictures and feelings
in the cells themselves. Like a sponge filled with water,
anywhere the flesh is pressed, wrung, even touched lightly,
a memory may flow out in a stream."*

-Clarissa Pinkola Estes, PhD

Contents

Art by Kat Shaw

Introduction and Welcome

"We are the Tree of Life. Our path is not up and out but in and through."
– *Kay Louise Aldred*

Welcome to your birth rite; the wisdom of your flesh and your shamanic ancestral spiritual heritage. Even if you know nothing about these things, science, particularly nervous system and trauma research, is currently studying somatic memory and intelligence and gaining more insight into this right now. In addition, you will undoubtedly have a forebear who was a shaman, as all cultures have shamans and the fact that you are here reading this now indicates that they are calling you to connect. Perhaps your ancestor was not known by that name but was considered as one who could 'see and know' nonetheless. We all have a seer and knower in our lineage and this predecessor is just waiting for us to remember them.

The purpose of *Somatic Shamanism* is for you to access your fleshy knowing and in doing so, release blocked energy, emotion and sensation – and so improve all aspects of your health and wellbeing: physical, mental, emotional, social, and spiritual. The added benefit is that through this you also gift liberation to, and improve the wellness of, your ancestral lines. As traditional shamanic teaching suggests, what you resolve for yourself you do for seven generations before and seven generations ahead. You no longer repeat and instead you repair.

This workbook is written from a trauma-informed and nervous system friendly perspective. *Somatic Shamanism* is a practice undertaken in a grounded, non-bypassing, and safe way. There are no 'peak' experiences to be found in the pages, and no dissociation-inducing activities. This book advocates for a sustainable spiritual discipline which does not dysregulate your nervous system and instead supports you to befriend and soothe your nervous system and release any survival stress – be that yours or ancestral – in a titrated, supported way.

Shamanism is the life path of one who knows. The Tree of Life is the entryway of connection and travel whilst journeying. In the case of *Somatic Shamanism*, the entry point is the body. Somatic means *of the flesh* and so this shamanic process cultivates your own 'fleshy knowing'. The foundational premise of this book is that the direction of travel is in and through not up and out of the body. This is a path of tangible divinity.

Why this book and these topics?

Shamanism, I believe, is the path which unites humankind. It is a way of living which is healing and based on a symbiotic relationship of deep reverent reciprocity with bodies – the body of the earth, our bodies and the bodies of all sentient beings. All bodies contain spirit, energy, and lifeforce, and shamanic practice supports us to see that extraordinary dimension of reality within the ordinary: flesh and bone, mud and rock, tree and plant, bird and fish, and so on. Shamanic principles are non-dogmatic, non-doctrinal and non-prescriptive, enabling individual cultures and people to formulate their own approach and expression.

Although I have 'trained' in shamanic healing (my teacher received her training via The Four Winds) I do not call myself a shaman. Neither would I call myself a neo-shaman. I am one who knows through my body, and it is the knowing through the body – *Somatic Shamanism* – which this book is providing a framework for.

As a seeker I have looked for the meaning of being alive and a felt sense experience of 'divinity' or 'spirit' in many places, modalities, religions and spiritual paths. I searched for it within orthodox Christianity for over 35 years which kept divinity as a logical concept only and outside of me – unobtainable in the messiness of human embodiment and bound by rules, accessible only through prescribed words and 'good works'. I then immersed myself in more 'new age' approaches – paying a lot of money and going up and out in high octane, nervous system blowing and dysregulating, dissociative, yogic, breathwork or meditative methods – blissing out but then still feeling empty, incomplete, heavy and disconnected, on a day-to-day basis.

Shamanism is an embodied path of one who knows, in their own way, and it was through embodiment, there, located within my own body – free of charge – where I found the knowing. Meaning and spirit were all within my own flesh and bone. I am offering you a map of how to find your way. I am aware that without the initial introduction to Peruvian indigenous shamanic tradition via Alberton Villoldo and the Four Winds, it might have perhaps taken me longer to get there. I know that I have colluded, unconsciously, with colonial and cultural appropriation, capitalist, and consumerist approaches to spiritual seeking, seduced by the aesthetic, the group think, and the spiritual entrepreneur marketed promise of healing and belonging – and for that I am sorry and have some shame and deep regret. Now that I am educated, I see that knowing – my own ancestral shamanic practice and lineage – was within me all along and that the indigenous cultures have and continue to be abused and used by western consumers wanting to have a quick fix or high (as the rise in plant medicines testify to) and who take, package, and sell their teachings as their own. That was not and is not my intention.

I am not doing that in this book. This book is a stimulus – steps and a method – for uncovering your own shamanic heritage and fleshy knowing. It contains creative activities for you to remember and uncover that and therefore your shamanic self. The exercises – the how and when – will arise organically from within you. This process involves unravelling from the cult of 'consuming a connection to spirit from the outside' and unravelling from the cults of 'guru', 'money', 'dogma' and 'doctrine'.

What you do with the knowing will also unfold. For me I can see and navigate energetic patterns and structures intuitively and instinctively – through my body and sensation – not through my human physical eyes. I had been doing this since birth. This for me is *Somatic Shamanism*, and my education around the nervous system has shown me, that my ability to do this is supersized and amplified due to being neurodivergent and having had significant trauma.

I am autistic and see in patterns – plus, as the Māori word for autism, *Takiwatanga* translates, those with autism are 'in his/her/their own time and space' and so are naturally, perhaps, seeing the patterning of the ordinary in alternative ways. Trauma can compromise energetic boundaries, break us open, and mean we can feel and see more deeply. Resolving trauma, feeling sensation more deeply, expanding my nervous system capacity and regulation led to, as I wrote in my book *Making Love with the Divine*, 'a sudden expansion of perception – working in accordance with my embodied knowing – resulted in a comprehension and felt sense of the immanence of the Divine.' Plus, 'my discovery is that all I seek and 'petition' the Divine for – including oneness, acceptance, gratitude, protection, safety companionship and belonging – are natural states of nervous system health and trauma resolution.'

Everybody has the ability to track energy as everyone has intuition and instinct. It's a fully embodied experience, not a dissociative one, and for that reason I write this book from a nervous system friendly and trauma informed lens. I have created, taught and facilitated a model which I call *Somatic Shamanism*. The journeying path moves us not only beyond the rational and logical and into the liminal and unconscious realms of the mind, but it also moves us into and through the wisdom of the body, as the Tree of Life. Intention is taken to the liminal and intuitive realm of the body – spirit within – to our fleshy knowing. There is no petitioning to Spirit – up and out of the body.

How does *Somatic Shamanism* fit with other religions and spiritual traditions?

Somatic Shamanism is not religion or a spiritual doctrine – there is no God or Goddess to pray to. Instead, there is a focus on connecting to the 'spirit', or lifeforce source of embodiment, and the creator or source origin of all that lives. It is animistic, in that it supports the notion that all things have 'soul' and are animated by a source energy, and pantheistic in that it promotes the idea that all (pan), or everything, is divine and alive with spirit or lifeforce (theos – God) and co-exists and relates. As the saying goes 'as above, so below, as within, so without' and the converse is true. Symbiosis or mutuality is the worldview – everything and everyone interrelates, including flesh and spirit. It works with the idea that spirit is within all aspects of nature and creation – everything is sacred and there is great power within the earth.

To emphasise again, *Somatic Shamanism* is not a religion, and I would argue, does not disrupt or disturb existing religious belief – indeed it compliments and has an interfaith component. World religions honour the sacredness of nature, and the Tree of Life is a symbol and metaphor common to them all. Speaking from my own religious background, Christianity, the Tree of Life is central to the creation narrative in Genesis. The Bible has animist aspects (wind as the breath of God, bird messengers – think Noah and the dove) and one could argue Jesus was shamanic. He shapeshifts and works with energy, when walking on water, turning water into wine, healing the blind, raising Lazarus from the dead. Within the history of Christianity, a mystical tradition can be unearthed where mystics entered trance, ecstatic and rapture states, directly communing with God through their bodies and felt sense, in dance for example and nature.

What is the process and how is it delivered?

Within *Somatic Shamanism,* I blend my own academic and experiential learning from theology, spirituality, shamanism, eroticism, somatics, energy medicine, neurosensory practices, priestessing, and the theological concept of the 'word becoming flesh.' It is a creative procedure, and I would encourage you to draw on your existing knowledge and learning, beliefs and modalities. Nothing is excluded.

Intention is the most important starting point as energy follows intention. My intention in writing this workbook was to catalyse others to discover their fleshy knowing – to live sacred and grounded existence in synchronicity with the earth – expansive, connected, intuitive and instinctive – with a felt sense of divine imminence and spirit within their mind, body and energy.

The process is not culturally specific – each culture has its own shamanic path and wheel anyway and you can research your legacy if you want to. The steps are prompts and building blocks, so you can tailor, uncover and rediscover your own path. You will make your own shamanic wheel according to whatever resonates – wicca, seasons, religious festivals, or nature's rhythms. Your body and nature are one so we will also look at including the four elements and directions and the parts of your body itself, head, torso, left, right and heart at the centre.

Using this book, you will tune in and receive guidance from your own shamanic self – one who knows – and later your ancestral wisdom. You will choose archetypes, animals, guides, helpers and allies – based on qualities, skills and values you'd like to learn and experience. Religious or spiritual figures you are already connected with might be part of this for you. Equally, fictional beings and characters in films, books and myths might also support you. You will journey through your body, supporting the containment of your nervous system and practices to ensure you stay in and through, not up and out, via rhythm, sound and movement supporting a safe change to your conscious state – for example, through drumming, rattling, walking, pacing or running, tapping, pendulating, swaying left to right and right to left, singing or chanting.

You will practise listening and learning from the intelligence of body, with your hands of light and looking through the eyes in your palms.

Finally, it is really important to hold on to critical thinking and using a variety of data, methods or sources to verify findings and what you learn. *Somatic Shamanism* is a path of fleshy knowing which involves listening to mind, body, energy, thought, sensation and intuition. Jung said we need the conscious to interpret and make sense of the unconscious. The reason why consciousness exists, and why there is an urge to widen and deepen it, is very simple: without consciousness things go less well.[1] I would also add that the heart can be a good arbitrator between mind and body, conscious and unconscious, logic and intuition.

---

[1] Carl Jung, CW 8, par. 695.

Before you Start

To remind you again, this is *your* journey, a recovery of your fleshy knowing and so you don't need to be 'trained.' This book provides a framework and prompts – it ignites and catalyses. Nothing is essential but it may be useful to gather and have in advance:

- different coloured pens and pencils
- different sizes and types of paper
- scissors, glue, old magazines
- a notebook
- stones
- objects from nature such as shells, leaves, sticks, stones, a candle, matches
- access to the internet

None of this is mandatory. However, as you are about to undertake a journey of internal shamanic self-discovery. What is essential is your commitment to this. Then prepare and reflect.

Start by thinking about your thinking:

Why and for what purpose are you reading this book?

What do you think about shamanism?

Who taught you this?

Are your ideas actually your own? If not, where do they come from?

Are you willing to let go of being told what to think and do spiritually and religiously – and instead be taught by the spirit of the body?

What is your primary intention for undertaking this journey? Write it down here:

Then think about your understanding of the book's key words:

- Somatic
- Shamanism
- Fleshy
- Knowing
- Tree of Life

How do you define them? Are the definitions your own or something you have inherited?

Next, notice your body's responses to the above. *Is it different than your mind's response?*

Does your body's reaction tell you something different than your thoughts?

Are there any surprises?

The journey of this book is about exploration, curiosity and discovery. You will get out of this year what you give. All that is really needed from you is your time, commitment, and willingness to reflect – listening to your mind, body and heart. You cannot do this wrong. You cannot get it wrong. Your own fleshy knowing and what you experience through your body as the Tree of Life, this is your truth. That is the learning.

Definitions

Before you read this content, please ensure you have read the *Before You Start* section of the book where you are asked to define some of these words for yourself. Your own definitions and understanding may well change as you move through the workbook or even immediately, after you have read this page. However, it is always wise and empowering to self-reference and defer to your own responses and inner knowing first. Start simultaneously centred in your own experience, thoughts and knowing, whilst remaining curious and open to amendment and adaptation.

These are the working definitions and explanations of the workbook's key terms:

Allies – helpers and supporters for mutually impactful outcomes.

Archetype – original pattern, model or energy structure.

Axis Mundi – pole or line connecting below and above, earth and cosmos, lower and upper worlds.

Breath – inspiration, life.

Consciousness – awareness, perception, responsive to surroundings.

Embodiment – tangible, incarnation, form.

Fleshy – part of the body, soft parts of an animal.

Four Directions – north, south, west and east.

Four Elements – earth, air, water, fire.

Knowing – full awareness, knowledge or consciousness.

Middle World – earth, consciousness, middle, torso.

Myth – story with a deeper meaning which explains a world view.

Power Animals – the energetic force of animals which we embody and receive support from.

Shamanism – life path and practice of one who knows.

Somatic – of the flesh.

Spirit – lifeforce, that which animates.

Spirit Keeper – guardians.

Trance – altered state of consciousness in response to external stimuli.

Tree of Life – main archetype of world religions, philosophies, myth and spiritual paths, representing growth and evolution. In this book the Tree of Life is the soma (body) and the entry point of connection and travel when journeying.

Underworld – unconscious, otherworld, spirit realm, below, legs and feet.

Upper World – cosmos, heaven, above, neck and head.

Wheel – circular process of the shamanic path.

Essential Understanding of the Nervous System, Stress and Trauma

Somatic Shamanism is a trauma-informed, nervous system friendly practise. So, let us begin firstly with the body, and more specifically, some basic education about the nervous system.

Understanding the nervous system and its functions, trauma, and trauma responses, are vital for safety and to prevent dissociation. It is also important to recognise and understand the stress and the stress responses of the body. In *Somatic Shamanism,* we hold the premise of 'first do no harm', as part of a trauma-informed approach.

Knowledge of the nervous system supports us to be less fearful of our own bodies, sensations, and reactivity. We become and remain embodied, and therefore, more able to access more fully our fleshy knowing, via intuition and instinct. It's only then that we can expand and relax into our living form and recognise that our bodies are doing their 'job' and are in fact only ever wanting to send us messages to keep us safe. We are then able to begin to trust our body, come into relationship with it, understand and accept our capacity moment to moment and meet our body's needs, self-soothe and self-care. The positive outcome of all of this is mastery, health and a deep connection with the wisdom held within our body messages and a complete and powerful embodiment of self.

When we anchor into embodiment, we incarnate, and we feel safer to be our creative and authentic self in the world. We are more able to access higher ordered thinking skills, creativity and intuition and are less likely to be subject to abuse, manipulation and control.

Embodiment is the FOUNDATION of fleshy knowing and our shamanic self. Once we are able to partner with our body, once we feel safe within it, we can access our innate gifts and independent thought and knowing.

So, what is the nervous system?

On the following page is a basic diagram based on Stephen Porges' Polyvagal Theory of the nervous system. Our nervous system has different parts.

The base of the diagram is the Ventral Vagal portion, the social engagement aspect of the nervous system. The place of safety, where we feel connected to others and our environment in the here and now. We are meant to live in this part of our nervous systems for the majority of the time. Here we are curious and here we LEARN. We rest and digest and our immune system works well.

The middle part of the diagram is the sympathetic portion, the fight, flight and what we also know now as the fawning aspect of the nervous system. This is activated in response to stress or a perceived threat. We need some sympathetic activation in our nervous system to support action and thinking but if we spend too long in activation, we start to experience an escalation of emotions and body symptoms, anxiety, and panic (flight, moving away from the threat), anger and rage (fight, moving towards the threat aggressively) and merging with others' views and people pleasing (fawn). Blood pressure, heartbeat and adrenaline increases, pupils dilute, we feel sweaty, digestion and immunity slow down, and we feel less connected to others. We can't fully access high order thinking skills here and creativity and intuition are impaired.

Finally, if we feel we cannot escape the stress of threat we move into freeze, the dorsal vagal aspect of our nervous system. Here the body immobilises and collapses. We are completely overwhelmed, feel helpless, numb, depressed, and can dissociate. In freeze we also shut down, heartbeat, blood pressure, body temperature, eye contact, immunity, social connection decrease. We feel shame, trapped – and the body prepares for death. Impactful shamanic journeying cannot take place here – memory and thinking is impaired, and creativity can't be accessed.

The action of the nervous system is incremented so we flow up from social engagement through flight, fight, fawn to freeze and then back down through fight, flight, fawn (deactivating) to social engagement. Sometimes in extreme threat, or in response to a stressor which feels life threatening due to a previous experience (a trauma response) we go from ventral vagal to dorsal vagal immediately. In coming out of freeze we do however move through the flight, fight, freeze deactivation.

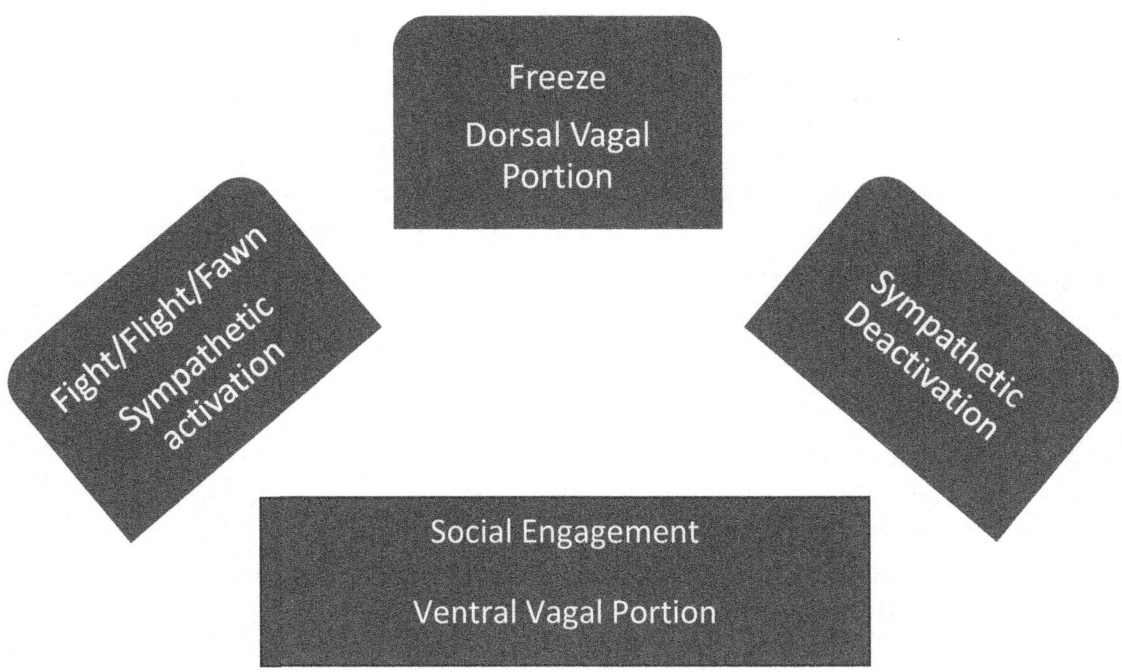

What is stress?

A stressor is *the trigger* for the activation of the body's (the nervous system sympathetic portion) stress response. The aim is to recognize the activation and our body's preferred way of responding whether it be flight, fight, fawn, freeze and to stay present to it, taking steps to both manage and reduce it, using the *mind* AND *body*.

What is our body's preferred stress response or responses?

Knowing ourselves is powerful. Tending to our preferred stress responses is self-care and I would argue, a spiritual practise. Most of us have a combination of responses and find we have different responses with different people or situations.

Are you a fighter? Do you have an explosive temper? Are you bullying, controlling, entitled, perfectionist when stressed?

Are you flight responsive? Do you experience obsessive and compulsive behaviours, anxiety, and perfectionism? Are you constantly doing and moving, worrying, and working?

Are you a fawner? Are you unable to express yourself and are manipulated or controlled by others? Do you rarely use the word I? Are you a yes person, a people pleaser, tending, soothing, and caring constantly for others, without standing up for your own views, needs and preferences?

Are you a freezer? Do you prefer hibernating rather than socialising and want to hide from reality? Do you experience spacey sensations, feeling unreal, isolation, brain fog and difficulties making decisions?

So, what are your go-to responses? Knowing them and working with exercises offered in the workbook will support your own nervous system to regulate and to bring you into the social engagement portion of the nervous system. This positively impacts on the quality of the shamanic experiences you have.

What is trauma?

Too much, too soon, too quickly.

Trauma is the reaction within the nervous system and brain, which occurs when someone does not have the capacity to stay present to an experience. The experience overwhelms us and takes us out of regulation.

Understanding trauma, yourself and working in a trauma-informed way supports you to stay in your window of tolerance (a term coined by Dan Siegal to describe the boundaries of emotional 'arousal' a person can cope, exist and live within without becoming overwhelmed) and regulation, so that you stay safely in your body, do not become overwhelmed or become traumatised or retraumatised further. Our trauma responses tend to follow the same pattern as our stress responses.

Importance of the Vagus Nerve

The vagus nerve is the primary nerve of the parasympathetic nervous system and balanced wellness and cognitive functioning. The strength and tone of this nerve impacts on resilience and emotional regulation and therefore, ability to connect, trust, digest information and learn. This nerve can be less 'toned' because of adverse childhood experiences (ACE) and trauma.

What can we do to support nervous system regulation and support the body to become more resilient to stress, expanding our own capacity?

Knowing your capacity, pacing, and taking self-responsibility are vital. Working within the boundaries of your nervous system, titrating experiences, and information, going slow, knowing less in more, allowing for digestion and integration of content and knowledge and sensation is how we expand and empower our body wisdom. Expanding capacity comes from being able to slow down, being able to track sensation, which is how the body communicates with us, and listen to its assessments and messages – responding to them supportively – signalling safety to the body.

The more capacity we build the more we can journey more deeply in and through our body – the Tree of Life, and access ancestral wisdom.

Map of the Journey

Somatic Shamanism: Your Fleshy Knowing as the Tree of Life

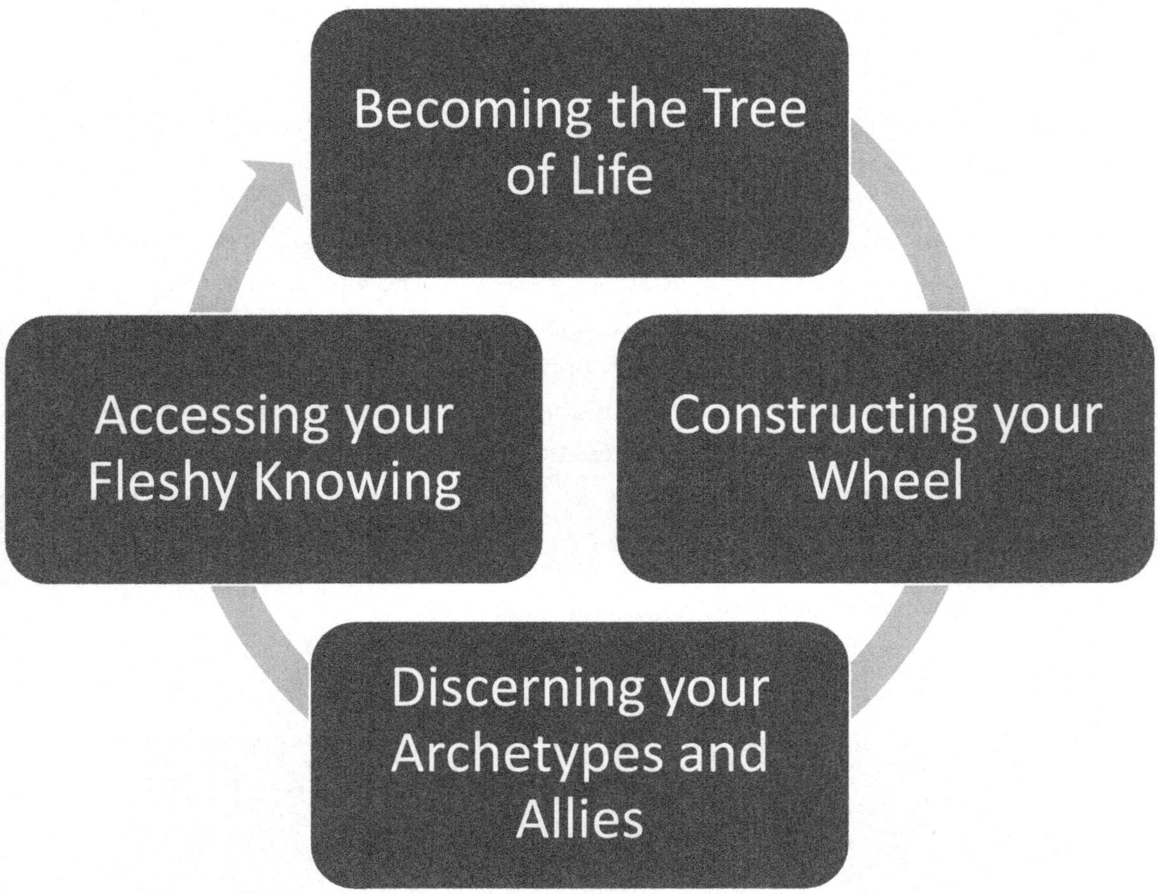

How to Use this Book

Having now seen a visual representation of the *Somatic Shamanism: Your Fleshy Knowing as the Tree of Life* (see *Map of the Journey on previous* page) you can see that it is a four-step process:

- Becoming the Tree of Life
- Constructing your Wheel
- Discerning your Archetypes and Allies
- Accessing your Fleshy Knowing

You will already have reflected on your understanding of Shamanism, what your intention is for embarking on this journey of fleshy knowing and made a commitment to be curious (see the *Introduction and Welcome* and *Before your Start* pages).

You can work through the book on your own, with a friend or in a group. Move through the four steps in the order and stages as listed and set out in the book.

You can start at any time of the year. You will need time to absorb, reflect and integrate so try not to race ahead. This is a different way of discovering, understanding and experiencing the world, your body and consciousness. It is an exploration of your whole self – your body, mind and spirit – and one that is led primarily by your body and lifeforce, not your mind. This is not the usual way of learning so it might feel odd.

How you access your fleshy knowing and how you undertake your shamanic journeys will be unique to you, most likely different than others, including your friends, so, if possible, stay away from comparison. There is nothing really 'to do' other than be open and receptive – to Spirit and your ancestral wisdom moving within and through you.

Your inner shamanic self and ancestral lineage will offer insight and direction, along with any other archetypes and allies, you call upon. This book is a structured way to catalyse and ignite what is within you and so it is a stimulus, an instruction book of 'how to' rather than a textbook of 'knowledge.' Trust and listen to yourself, the internal teacher who whispers (and sometimes shouts), and your fleshy knowing (sensation, impulse and feelings).

Finally, please note shamanic practise of any sort is not advised for anyone taking mind or consciousness altering drugs. None of the information presented in this book is meant to replace the advice of a medical, health, legal and/or any other professional or service. How you choose to act on the words and content is of your own determination and free will. If at any point you feel comfortable with what you are experiencing, then stop.

Dedication

I dedicate this book to:

- **Matter** – 'the stuff from which the universe is made' – solid, gases and liquids.
- **Energy** – that which animates.
- **Trees** – our greatest teachers – that offer a visual demonstration of the mystery of the wheel.
- **Allied and archetypical energy** – thank you.
- **Bodies** – through somatic ecstatic experience consciousness finally 'sees all'.

May we:

- Go in and through.
- Connect to our fleshy knowing.
- Sanctify animal, mineral, plant, fungi, bacteria.

Art by Sophie Skinner

Chapter 1: Become the Tree of Life

"Earth my body
Water my blood
Air my breath
Fire my spirit."

– *Origin Unknown*

What is the Tree of Life?

The Tree of Life is a symbol and metaphor which has a place in most of the main world religions, spiritual paths and philosophical traditions. The main concept it represents is the connection of the *lower world* – the depths of the earth – the place of the dead, spirits, ancestors and soul and the *upper world* – the cosmos – the place of celestial dwelling – heaven. So, the tree is the channel through which lifeforce – energy – flows. Each culture has its own interpretation of this sacred symbol.

The main motifs of the Tree of Life are that of connectivity, solidity, evolution and rebirth. The tree is a bridge, pole, or a connective channel. The roots deeply embed into the earth and draw lifeforce from the fertile compost of 'death', moving it up through the solid pole trunk and the branches, to the leaves, facilitating their budding, unfurling and blooming, until it reaches the higher realms. From these sky and cosmic realms there is a flow of inspiration, an airy and solar energy, which supports photosynthesis and therefore life here in the physical realm. Through inspiration there is a regenerating and cascading outpouring of life supporting energy into the earth's atmosphere, which flows down to the earth and supports the lifegiving power of leaves. In the autumn as leaves shed, there is a composting which provides the foundations for rebirth and the cycle to begin again. This creates a circular energy flow of death, rebirth, life, of flourishing, decay, gestation and so on.

In addition, 'the tree' is a place of both strength and reliability and serenity and peace. It is a living haven which offers restoration and recuperation. Also, the symbol of the 'family tree' is a roadmap of branches to our ancestors. It links us to our heritage and roots. It is again a symbol of universal connection and immortality, in that despite death our ancestral line continues. We are a continuation of those which have gone before – birthed from the composted leaves of their lives.

The Tree of Life, although a symbol of universal linking, is also a symbol of unique individuality. These two apparent oppositional symbols paradoxically coexist in relation to the Tree of Life. The genus of trees – species of physical trees – are numerous in their variety, just as there are many different religious, spiritual and philosophical traditions. However, there remains one ultimate source and creator – the Tree of Life itself – which is seen through the prism of different religious, spiritual and philosophical teachings and beings. That is why shamanism is universal – and the symbol on which it is based is also universal and unifying.

The origins of the symbol can be traced, as said earlier, to every tradition and civilisation so it may interest you to research your own. My own ancestral tradition is that of Celtic Christianity. Within Christianity, the Tree of Life is obvious and explicit within the Genesis creation story (Genesis Ch 2) – where it holds keys to the door of gnosis and universal knowledge of good and evil. It is written into the narrative as a motif of the original unification of humanity and divinity.

From the Celtic perspective, the Tree of Life is a symbol of wisdom and balance – and the access point to the spirit realm. It creates a harmonious linking amongst nature's forces and connects heaven and earth in a never-ending circle of life, death and rebirth. The Celts deeply revered nature and so had a variety of trees which were considered sacred. For me, the Hawthorn and Holly are the two which resonate most.

Other names for the Tree of Life are *Tree of Knowledge, Tree of Creation, World Tree, Universal Tree* and *Cosmic Tree*. Charles Darwin also wrote on the symbol of the Tree of Life in *On the Origin of the Species* stating that 'the affinities of all the beings of the same class have sometimes been represented by a great tree. I believe this simile largely speaks the truth.' So, through this image, evolution and the relationship between all current living or extinct things, can be, according to Darwin, considered and examined.

What is the Axis Mundi?

The Tree of Life is also one interpretation of the axis mundi. The axis mundi is the line around which something rotates. In the case of the earth, the Tree of Life can be considered the axis mundi – the column trunk connects the roots deep into the centre of the earth and to the branches reaching high into the sky – the cosmos. It is a symbol common to shamanic traditions and for the purposes of this book and the tree being our bodies, this makes us the axis mundi. We become the channel, the pole, through which the energy flows. This requires us to 'hollow out' and become, what traditional shamanism calls 'a hollow bone', a bridge connecting earth and cosmos and a vessel through which energy and messages can flow. This is a strong energy and that is why it is important to work in a nervous system friendly and trauma-informed way, at the pace and capacity of your own system.

What can we learn shamanically from observing a physical tree?

Observing a physical tree for one entire year – touching and communing with it through the seasons of the year – is a deep learning experience. We can observe how it connects above and below, the sky and earth, reaches high and low, and moves energy from branches to root and back again. Learning about and feeling into sap flow educates us in how energy flows in a shamanic sense.

Watching a seed fall from a tree, implant naturally into the compost of the fallen leaves (the shedding and old growth which has died and decomposed) and then observing the shoots of life springing forth from the rot and a tree sapling grow, fosters and cultivates within us a visceral knowing of the potentiality of intention and the power of earth and cosmos working together. We learn that trees regenerate and create ancestral lineage. The first *Try This* activity of the workbook is below. It is about the importance of connecting to a physical tree during your first journey around the shamanic wheel.

***Try This:* Trees as Teachers**

Part 1: Reflection and Research Task

Ask yourself now what species of tree is your favourite and why?

That which you choose can tell you a lot about your shamanic self.

My choice would be Hawthorn – native to my Celtic ancestral origins. You may have another choice. Tree symbology and meaning can be researched, but it is interesting for you to initially reflect on what the tree means to you before you look it up. When I think of a Hawthorn tree I think of the (often hidden from sight) thorns and the learning they gift me – that all of nature and all living things need to be handled with gentleness, care and respect or there will be consequences! Hawthorn trees are resilient, self-protective – and very beautiful in blossom in spring and then when red berried in autumn. The berries are heart medicine and so this tree with its thorns and bright blossom, for me, encapsulates the energy of all of life – pain, beauty, and love.

Research has offered me further insight into my favourite tree. In paganism and Celtic mythology, the Hawthorn tree symbolises fertility, protection, and magic – fairies are thought to guard the tree. It is a goddess tree – encapsulating maiden, mother crone.

Reflect on the tree you chose and then do so research to find out more about the myths which surround it and which medicine it offers.

Part 2: 12-Month Tree Observation

Walk around your local area and choose a physical tree to observe. This will be your physical representation of the Tree of Life.

Be drawn to its energy – it will identify itself to you. Then watch it closely for a full 12 months and see what you learn. I would suggest that each season you do the following:

- Touch and hug the tree (asking permission first of the tree and its spirit keeper, see below) and track and reflect on how it feels each season. *What are the changes?*

- Get to know this tree well – draw it, paint it, photograph it. Document how it changes and what that means for you. You can draw your tree on the page that follows. Note your initial observations below:

- When you visit and hug it, 'listen' to its voice and its heartbeat. As you do this more frequently, you will experience shapeshifting (taking on shape and form) and merging with it and become one Tree of Life together. Note your initial observations below:

- As you learn from the tree, journal about it. This is integral to *Somatic Shamanism* and connecting to your fleshy knowing – as you are the Tree of Life. Note your initial observations below:

Draw your Tree

As with your favourite species of tree in **Part 1** you can identify the type of tree it is and research the symbolism, medicine and meaning of the tree if you'd like to – but only after you find one which calls to you intuitively and instinctively.

Finally, a note about *permission*. Each tree has its own sacred spirit keeper – a being or energy which guards the tree. After you have observed the tree a few times you will get a sense of who or what this is. If you are not sure, you can imagine or journal about a gate in front of the tree and who holds the keys to this. Or draw the gate in front of the tree and who holds the keys. Trust what you see, feel and know. The spirit keeper will reveal themselves clearly as they are the guardian of the tree's energy.

Spirit keepers of trees come in all sorts of shapes, sizes, gender and forms – from fairies to green men, to animals and goddess, ancestors, and humans who lived in the area in earlier centuries. Sometimes it can be an element – wind or fire, a shape, mythical being or fictional character. It is important to identify them if you ask their permission to approach the tree – and also ask for guidance from them about the concept of the tree of life, what it means to embody the energy and the magic of trees.

How are You the Tree of Life?

You are the Tree of Life – the pole between earth and cosmos – the axis mundi. Your body is this pillar. As the universal energy flows through, you are able to see the universe and your body are one – reflections of each other – as within, so without – Earth my body, Water my blood, Air my breath and Fire my spirit (*Origin Unknown).* Our body contains everything – life, death, rebirth, wisdom of past, present and future and when we activate our shamanic self and shapeshift our body into the Tree of Life, we are able to access our eternal self, fleshy knowing and spiritual, internal sight.

How this is activated, the ability to connect to fleshy knowing, is usually following a major life event and in traditional shamanism after a period of suffering which opens us up to deeper sensation (after illness and pain) and feeling and emotion (after trauma, suffering or intense joy). Activation of fleshy knowing comes after an awakening.

Once we connect to ourselves as The Tree of Life – we feel and know our roots, our ancestors and we connect to the alchemy and magic of our sun self, moon self, star self, fruit, bird, animal, plant, fire, water, air and spirit selves and release the belief that is separation between us and them. We also learn that our organs have spirit keepers and that we are directly connected to mythical beings. Indeed, that we are spirit, god, goddess – our flesh is them.

Our bodies are a channel in the middle world and link cosmos and earth, upper and lower worlds. Our brain and its neurons form the branches of the tree and are how our shamanic self can access the highest perspectives and an overview of world – offering insight and guidance to our 'inner community' i.e., to other parts of self (inner parts) which may cause internal struggle due to having conflicting views, wants, likes and dislikes. Our torso is the trunk of the tree, our stability and embodied wise self, living in the middle world, in the here and now. Our heart is at the centre. Our lower abdomen and base of our torso is the gateway from which our roots – which are our legs and feet – anchor us into the earth. The area from which we shed, expel and compost – our anus – is how we access ancestral wisdom and the underworld. More about this later in the workbook.

***Try This:* Transforming your Body into The Tree of Life**

Shapeshift into the Tree of Life now – using the breathing, movement, and visualisation sequence below. Repeat this daily for at least ten days consecutively each season, ideally outside by the physical tree you have chosen to observe for 12 months.

- Breathe in – form your trunk – feel your belly and chest inflate and stabilise and strengthen. Open your heart.
- Breathe out – send your roots down, connect into the earth.
- Breathe in and connect to the lifeforce energy of the earth and bring it through your feet and legs to the base of your torso.
- Breathe out – send the earth lifeforce through your body into your mind.
- Breathe in and feel branches and buds growing – see the neuron wiring of your brain sparking and the leaves of your tree blooming.
- Breathe out – lengthen the branches and open the leaves – stretching out your arms and opening the palms to face upwards.
- Breathe in the energy of sun through your palms, creating flowing sap, and send this down your arms into your trunk.
- Breathe out sap and sun energy into earth and shedding of leaves – shake your palms and feet.

Art by Sophie Skinner

Chapter 2: Construct your Wheel

"Shamans taught me that black is the colour of the west on the medicine wheel, the direction linked to earth, the female body, introspection, change, death and intuition."
– *Connections, Gabrielle Roth*

The Wheel

Each Shamanic tradition has its own wheel – a map of the sacred path taken, and a symbol of life cycles – the descent and ascent journey and aspects of reality, wellness, and the universe. The wheel represents entirety, completion, and a never ending, eternal, movement of beginnings, endings, and beginnings. It is a metaphor for the journey of the human life cycle too.

How the wheel is constructed, and the elements included within it varies. The wheel is culturally adapted to the belief system, worldview, environment, and the traditions of the people working with it. Therefore, you are invited to design your own – a wheel which holds meaning for you and which represents your own background, beliefs, culture, and traditions.

Building your wheel is a creative process and one which will evolve and will likely be subject to change. It is not a once and for all time activity and you can't get it wrong. It is a trial-and-error experience. It is messy and organic. It arises from embodied knowing, sensation, observation of the natural world, and from what resonates with you – your preferences and passions. It is a *symbol of meaning* for you. For this reason, nothing is excluded. You are welcome to include and draw on your cultural experiences, religious background and what feels right for you in your body. Nothing is 'out of bounds' or forbidden.

The ideas below are prompts and suggestions. They are based on my own personal experience and research. The reason why it is important to create a wheel, is so you have a visual representation of your embodied knowing – and because of this the body relaxes into the journey as it knows where it is going. The wheel, at first, is simply a theoretical concept but as you journey around it throughout the whole year it will become alive and so will develop deeper meaning and representation for you. As I have already said you may find it completely changes.

I've journeyed around many wheels – medicine wheels (based on Peruvian shamanic lineage and The Four Winds and Celtic shamanism), the Christian calendar wheel, the Wiccan wheel of the year and the sabbats, the Rose Lineage priestess wheel based on the Venus cycle and myth of Inanna, the wheel of the elements (earth, air, fire, water, metal), chakra cycles and energy bodies, the astrological wheel... to name a few. What I've discovered is that the wheel I journey round now, year-on-year morphs – it's not static – and is based on what feels true to me at that moment.

I was searching for a meaning to the rhythm of my life and found it in listening to my own embodied experience, connecting to my ancestral roots and the environment in which I live. This also felt the most aligned ethically as it reflected my personal heritage and value system and avoided cultural appropriation. Surprisingly, my wheel is now very basic, and I will share with you below what I feel are the core elements of most shamanic wheels and from that you can flesh out your own.

There are four sections of the wheel – quadrants – each which have symbols, qualities, skills and attributes designated to them. How you assemble this will be based on your own embodied rhythm and instinct. I have listed qualities and attributes in groups and from that you can decide which (if any) resonate with you and assign them into the quadrant which feels right to you mixing and matching them with attributes from other groupings. You do *not* have to include each grouping in your wheel. Which attribute goes with another if entirely based on your own fleshy knowing – your intuition. There are groupings below to offer inspiration to you.

Core Element 1: The Wheel and the Tree of Life

The two quadrants to the right of the vertical line represent the *waxing* part of the year – Dec to June (budding to full bloom) and to the left the *waning* part of the year – June to Dec (harvest to fall and decomposition). The two quadrants above the horizon represent the centre of the tree trunk, *branches* and canopy of leaves, and the two quadrants below the horizon represent the base of the trunk and the tree *roots*. You might like to draw your tree through the middle of the wheel.

Core Element 2: The Wheel and the Axis Mundi

As mentioned in the previous chapter, the axis mundi is the pillar of the world –the central line on which the world rotates and the column which connects cosmos, or *above,* and the earth, or *below*. This is the trunk of the tree and so in the wheel it is the vertical line running through the centre.

Core Element 3: The Wheel and your Body

The centre of the wheel – where the vertical and horizontal lines meet – is the centre of your body and the point where they exactly cross is your *heart* space. It is the point of balance, the place to which we return for the final say and guidance, and that which connects the direction of above – our *voice and mind* – to the direction of below – our *gut instinct and creative womb space*.

If you stand up – part your legs slightly and raise your arms above your head and part them slightly there – then you yourself make a wheel. Above your heart is the top of the trunk and the branches form from your mind and arms and hands. Below your heart is the base of the trunk, your legs and the roots are our feet. Some traditions say the left portion of the body, represents feminine energy and the ability to *be*, *receive* and *nurture* yourself and holds insight into emotions and health. In these traditions the right is the masculine energy, your ability to *do, create and form*, and is a representation of outer life and projects.

As your body syncs with the cycles of nature and trees, we start, end, and start again with the body, as well as the wheel and nature's cycles, over and over and over again.

Somatic Shamanism is not a pathway of up and out of the body. Your body is the container and the wheel itself, so you journey in and through the axis mundi – central pillar and column – the vertical line of the wheel which is your body itself and passed straight through the heart space.

This is the wheel of carnal wisdom and fleshy knowing.

Groupings and suggestions for the quadrants of the wheel you create

Groupings and suggestions for quadrants:

Below, Above, Within, Without

South, North, West, East

Middle world, Threshold, Underworld, Upperworld

Noon, Afternoon, Midnight, Morning

Sun, Moon, Dark, Light

Summer, Autumn, Winter, Spring

June, September, December, March

Yellow, Red, Black, White

Fire, Water, Earth, Air

Full Bloom, Shedding, Decomposing, Budding

Birth, Youth, Maturity, Death

Maiden, Lover, Mother, Crone

Ovulation, Pre-Menstrual, Bleed, Pre-Ovulation

December, March, June, September

Winter Solstice, Spring Equinox, Summer Solstice, Autumn Equinox

Dark Moon, Waxing Moon, Full Moon, Waning Moon

Underworld, Ascent Middle World, Upper World, Descent Middle World

Full Exhale, Inhale, Full Inhale, Exhale

Action, Completion, Rest, Ideas

Mind, Gut Instinct, Intuition, Creativity

Roots, Base of Trunk, Top of Trunk, Branches

Instinct, Inspiration, Eros, Intuition

Root Chakra, Sacral and Solar Plexus Chakra, Throat Chakra, Third Eye and Crown Chakra

Feet and Legs, Abdomen, Sternum and Voice Box, Brain

It is also possible to base your wheel quadrants on religious festivals.

You can add much more detail about any of the above – especially body organs.

Nature Objects and the Wheel

Throughout the year you will collect (and so associate) certain objects from nature with areas of the wheel and may well make a 3-D version of your wheel. Objects might correspond with the associations, attributes, and qualities you create on your paper wheel. Here are some examples:

Candle, Feather, Shell, Rock

Green Leaf, Acorn, Bare Twig, Bud

Rose in Bloom, Wilting Rose, Rose Hip, Rose Bud

Green Stone, Brown Stone, Grey Stone, Yellow Stone

You might also find an object which represents your heart and goes in the centre of the 3 D wheel you build.

Animals and the Wheel

Power animals are part of every wheel and shamanic journey. They tend to follow the four themes and so correspond with the quadrants and the collective associations, qualities and attributes of each quarter.

Animals of Winter – hibernation, protection, and wisdom – such as Wolf, Bear and Owl.

Animals of Spring – regeneration, inspiration, and spark – such as Deer and Hare.

Animals of Summer – action, exaltation, and regality – such as Hawk or Eagle.

Animals of Autumn – flow, cleansing, releasing – fish, e.g., Salmon or water-based animals, e.g., Otter.

The Central Archetype connected to the Wheel is The Serpent

If you are phobic of snakes, you are welcome to skip this section. If you're not it is especially useful to consider the archetype of serpent and the wheel. Central animal symbol to the concept of the wheel and cycle of life is the *ouroboros* – the snake which eats its tail. It a symbol of eternity – of death, rebirth, life, death, rebirth, life – never-ending circular action of a snake that eats its tail. And so, for me, the ouroboros serpent is the wheel itself. It forms the outer circle – shedding its skin year on year – as the journey around the wheel is completed once more. The Ouroboros is the circle of energy and forms the entire outer rim and so is the container and the matrix itself – continually moving in an eternal and endless cycle of regeneration and change. This is another reason why your wheel will morph and change. Nothing is static.

The snake/serpent, for me, is the gentlest and wisest archetype and power animal. It gifts us a gateway to the paradise of embodiment and from my perspective moves around the wheel changing form as it goes, keeping us connected and always working with our physical self and form. The snake and serpent are found in most spiritual and religious traditions, often in a misunderstood form. It is an ancient symbol of myths, predating religions and represents life and death simultaneously – and is, therefore, a perfect symbol for the wheel. Plus, evolutionary wise serpents are old in the timeline of living beings. They represent lifeforce – or the kundalini – the nervous system flow through the body. So, drawing a snake, coiling around and through your Tree of Life, your body, as or as part of the axis mundi, the trunk and pillar – connecting cosmos and earth – symbolises the flow of spirit, lifeforce, breath moving through the hollow bone you become as your shamanic self.

When I draw my wheel, I have the Ouroboros as the outer rim of the wheel, the serpent flowing through the centre of the trunk of my tree of life and my physical form, my torso. Plus, I have a form of serpent/snake as an archetype in each quadrant.

Winter – I have a *dragon serpent* – who breathes fire from the centre of the earth – keeping my roots in touch with lifeforce, whilst the tree is dormant and rests. Dragon serpent is the fire of digestion, elimination and an underworld ally.

Spring – I have *flying serpent* – who lives in my mind, retrieving sparky ideas and inspiration – creating buds of thought on the breaches of my tree.

Summer – I have *royal cobra* – which moves up my spine, helping me stand tall in my full bloom embodiment – a glorious array of skills and sharing gifts, seeing projects come to fruition, connecting to others.

Autumn – I have *water serpent* – who moves on the surface waters – shedding old skins, cooling the fire of winter, preparing for the descent to the roots and rest – creating a lightness for the journey.

If this resonates for you, or if you are in a part of the world where you know more about specific snakes and their qualities, consider if they need to be part of your wheel.

Archetypes and Allies and the Wheel

As you journey around the wheel and through your body, you will feel the presence of animals, archetypes and allies. Some will be familiar – coming from religious traditions and spiritual paths you are drawn to, have studied or are affiliated with, some will be new to you. With regards to archetypes and animals, constructing the wheel according to where you are in the world and what you see around you, your heritage and ancestry is a good place to start. Also, often, we have a strong connection to an ancestor, and they can turn out to be one of our most powerful allies.

If you already have a spiritual tradition or religion, you might like to add archetypes, spiritual beings and figures from these which are resonant or have meaning to you. For example, I have Mother Mary, Jesus, Mary Magdalene and Sophia on my wheel – all of which are biblical-based figures.

Furthermore, archetypes and allies can be fictional characters from books or superheroes/heroines. Examples being Professional McGonagall, Dumbledore, Hermione Grainger and Harry himself from the Harry Potter books, Superman and Wonder Woman from Marvel, Thor and Black Widow from Avengers. More about this later in the book.

It is also perfectly ok to add music as an ally, crystals, oils, food, herbs, clothing items, and places in the world to the quadrants. Be creative!

***Try This:* Constructing your Wheel**

Draw your wheel – there is a template for you to trace on the following page.

Draw your Tree of Life and body running through the centre – you will find space to do so after the wheel template.

Draw the ouroboros around the outer wheel ring – if that feels good for you to do so.

Include the serpent archetypes – as I described above – in the quadrants if (and only if!) resonant.

Add the core elements information to each quadrant (if they work for you) and then attributes, body parts, archetypes, allies and animals, to complete your wheel for the time being.

Remember

Start with a basic wheel and add to it as you go through the workbook, experience journeys and move through a year consciously connected to the seasons, life cycle of a tree and your body.

It's ok to change your mind and adapt, amend and change your wheel at any point.

Wheel Template

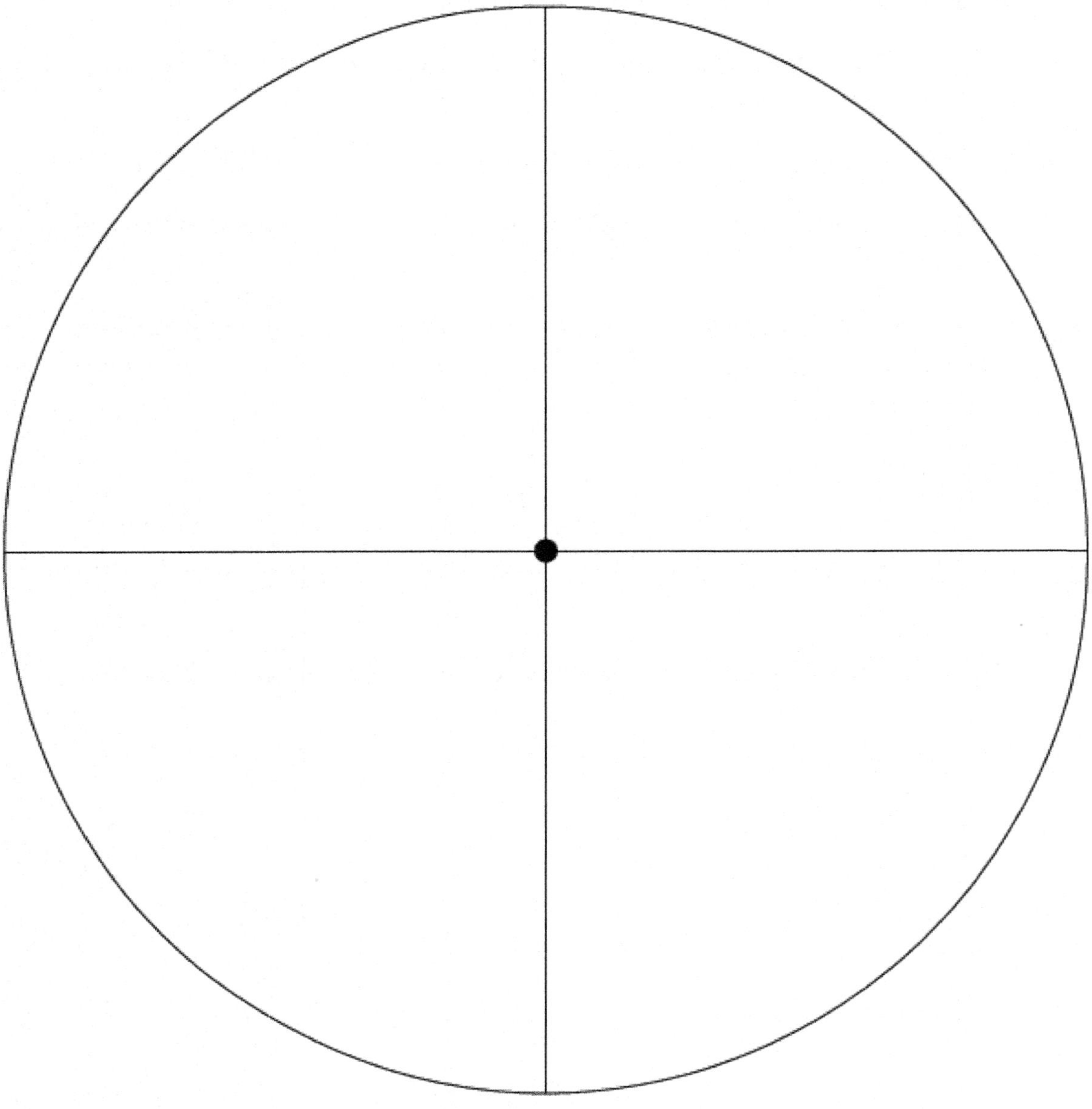

Draw your Tree of Life and body running through the centre.

Art by Sophie Skinner

Chapter 3: Discerning your Archetypes and Allies

"Archetypes resemble the beds of rivers: dried up because the water has deserted them, though it may return at any time. An archetype is something like an old watercourse along which the water of life flowed for a time, digging a deep channel for itself. The longer it flowed the deeper the channel, and the more likely it is that sooner or later the water will return."
– *Carl Jung*

Once you have constructed your wheel it is time to tune into yourself and discern which archetypes, allies and power animals are already present within you, which support both your shamanic self, as active soul parts – an expression of your lifeforce energy – within your mind, body and spirit, and your connection to the spirit realm. In addition to this, it is time for you to discern which archetypes, allies and powers are trying to connect and which *soul parts* (parts of lifeforce energy) are trying to return to you to embody and make manifest.

The origin and exactly what archetypes are is a bit of a mystery. Generally, it is accepted that archetypes are original ('arche' Greek) patterns, models, images or energy structures which exist in our mind, body, and energy fields and can be tapped into for guidance, expansion, and connection to self. They are structures of the psyche which are universal and eternal, and so hold both collective and ancestral memory, which help us to make sense of and meaning within the world.

Archetypes contain light and dark aspects, and both aspects need to be integrated, as they can't be changed or eradicated. Once given appropriate, safe, expression in our lives – usually most effectively through creativity and embodied free flow methods – they allow us to access empowering aspects of ourselves – emotionally, physically, socially and spiritually. Examples are our warrioress, queen or king, our sage or wisewoman, or inner goddess – but the list of archetypes is endless. How an archetype manifests, appears and is embodied, is different for each of us and an individual experience. The universal essence of each archetype might be similar across all cultures and humans, but stereotypical portrayal – especially gender specific ones – and logic, are not the purpose or energy of archetypes. Regardless of our assigned gender at birth we can possess all archetypes within us – including, mother and father, maiden and prince, hero and heroine. In the long run, integrated archetypes support us to gain compassionate connectedness, wholeness and a sense of completion.

Archetypes enjoin us to the energetic structures of the imaginal, mythic and spiritual realms, and so can be accessed through mythic stories and poetry, folklore or spiritual texts, alongside songs, images, art, drama and dreams. Some archetypes may carry similar patterning and energy across different traditions but be called by different names. For example, in some cultures, 'shaman' is an archetype of males, and the female equivalent is crone or wise woman. Other names for the archetype of shaman across the globe include witch, medicine man or woman, wizard, healer, sorcerer, seer, but these are only some examples. The key to finding your shamanic self is feeling into the energy, what it means for you, and how it expresses through you, your ancestral lineage and culture. It can take time for the name and what it looks like to become clear.

Myths are stories with a deeper meaning, which explain a world view. The route into archetypes via myth is not explicit. Archetypes come alive through lucid dreaming, imaginative activity, creativity and non-direct storytelling, which includes storytelling through ritual, dance and music. The language of archetypes is symbolic and metaphorical and so tapping into the wisdom is not done logically and rationally but rather via shamanic techniques, during which the mind moves into the intuitive, liminal and imaginal realms.

Archetypes might show themselves as allies and can appear to us in pairs, families or groups (think maiden, mother/lover, crone and queen and king), through visions and journeys by visually appearing in our mind's eye or in an embodied way, through which we may feel them present in our body, strengthening, healing or expanding our capacities. Equally, archetypal energy might appear to us in our dreams, art or writing in the form of a mythical being, religious figure, god, goddess, fictional comic, book or film character, in order to expand us energetically. As we feel their expansion in our energy field we might connect more deeply to spirit, source or the earth. In archetypically shapeshifting we might feel ourselves connecting directly to an archetype, ally or power animal and actually becoming it – Athena, Artemis, Mother Mary, Zeus, Cat Woman, Superman, for example. Shapeshifting can support us to behave differently, see alterative perspectives, move through blocks, and have more endurance, self-compassion or courage.

Archetypal energy in the body organically shows itself though spontaneous movement and sensation. Expansion in the chest, opening to more love may be Kuan Yin or Christ energy, and fire in the belly, self-protection, maybe Kali or Batman. Relating with archetypes is creative.

You can also call archetypes in. Ask to feel, see and know the presence of the archetype of kindness, bravery, wisdom and see what shows up for you. These become your allies – the helpers and supporters who work with you for mutually impactful outcomes, spirit guides and keepers – who are guardians of the realms and worlds, and also aspects of your body, during shamanic journeys – and yet are also in you – so you are simultaneously and perhaps paradoxically both an ally and companion for yourself.

Archetypal energy can also take the form of a power animal – which activates the energetic force of the animal within us so we can embody it and receive support from it. As mammals we, as humans, can receive a lot from coupling to our animal nature and shapeshifting into our animal ancestry and power. This is an integral part of *Somatic Shamanism* – the life path and practice of one who knows through the flesh (the soft parts of animal body).

Connecting to the power animal of lion, for example, can offer us empowerment and the roar of our boundaries. The serpent connects us to our lifeforce, our creativity, and eros helps us to shed old ways of being with ease. Connecting to elephant power animal gifts us stability and the ability to remove even the biggest and densest blocks in our lives. Giraffe helps us see above the drama and of course eagle, allows us to connect to spirit and see the bigger picture and highest perspective. Making the shapes and moving like (and as) these animals helps us to bridge and shapeshift more deeply into the archetypical energy of the power animal. This is done in trance states, or shamanic journeys through creative movement and dance. More about this later.

Allies and archetypes can also be found in the natural world. There are nature spirits such as the fae (mythical and supernatural nature beings, also known as fairies), spirits of trees, plants, the winds (shamanic traditions believe the winds from each direction have specific qualities, mentorship and properties) rocks, seas, and rivers. There are also nature deities of the sun, moon, other planets, the sky, water, fire, plus the earth herself as the goddess Gaia, and gods such as the oak or holly kings of pagan traditions. In addition, there are other nature and mythical beings found in folklore such as dragons, ogres, banshees, gnomes, goblins, mermaids, unicorns, minotaur, centaur, devas, werewolves, fauns, phoenix, griffin, loch ness monster, big foot plus many others. You will have beings and spirits native to your own culture and will be able to discern which feel like guides for you.

Objects from nature may be allies for you in that you feel they hold guidance or magical powers – energies which support your journey. These sacred objects may anchor energy, hold 'medicine' or 'magic' or be symbolic. Sticks may direct energy and expansion when held against the body. Holding a stick upright against the chest, vertically, may support the body to shapeshift into the trunk of the tree of life and become the axis mundi pillar. Holding a larger stick, to the ground, like a staff, again might help the body interface with the Tree of Life and feel grounded and banging the stick on the ground awaken awareness to the underworld. Stones of certain shapes and sizes can help conjoin us to the essence of what we nominate them to represent. For example, I have a black stone which I hold to ally with dark moon and a white one for full moon. Pinecones might support us as we hold it to shapeshift or commune to the spirit of the pine tree. Acorns or sycamore keys might hold the energy of new beginnings, womb seeds and potential. Equally animal bones might help us to connect to the shedding process or be an ally to evoke the presence and support of benevolent ancestors. The choice is endless, and it is about you discerning, listening to your intuition and following it without analysis. It's a lovely idea to have some cloth or a bag to hold any of these objects in.

A reminder – allies and archetypes can be both non-fictional or fictional – from stories, films and songs, and non-fictional, real people, teachers, good friends or ancestors past and present. Connecting to allies, guides and archetypes happens in the liminal and imaginal realms so nothing and none is out of bounds. Finally, these guides may arise from spiritual or religious lineages, disciplines and paths, alongside spirit realms and ancestral lineage. You may have gods, goddesses, spirits and teachers (living or dead) from paths and religions you are or have been affiliated with which feel present and a part of your spirit team. In addition, you can connect to other planetary, intergalactic beings, such as Pleiadean, Venusian, and angels.

The bottom line is that all the above energies, beings, archetypes, and allies are within you already.

Try This: **Discerning your Archetypes and Allies**

Archetypes are an aspect of source and spirit within us – inner helpers which are paradoxically indistinguishable from our psyche, DNA, flesh and blood. We are going to start by discerning and creating a core team of allies for your *Somatic Shamanism* toolkit, drawing on archetypes.

To do this you will need a **big piece of paper, pencil and pens of varying colours**.

On your paper **draw out the diagram on the next page**. These are some of the main archetypes Carl Jung believed we all contain within us.

What you are going to do is get to know how they appear and live within you so that you are not surprised when they turn up during shamanic journeys and can call on them for wisdom and guidance. Remember these already exist inside of you – you already have an inner shaman, child, queen, king (you have both regardless of gender), rebel, etc. – we are simply making them more conscious.

What the archetypes are is self-explanatory by the name – I don't want to define them for you as you will have your own image and idea of what they are and mean. However, to clarify, the masculine and feminine are the 'exalted' version of the archetypes, the inner and mature father king 'god' and mature mother queen 'goddess'. The shaman archetype is the part of you who 'knows' – holds wisdom – and finally, the Self is your wholeness, the contained and regulatory part of you which leads – so is quite an abstract aspect.

The key to this exercise is to create a *profile* of each archetype. This can be a list of words and sentences describing and listing the name, quality and skills of each archetype. Or it could be a mixture of words, sounds, images (cut out of magazines) or drawn. The archetype may be identical to a spiritual figure, being, nature object, colour, god, goddess, fictional character or it may be a mixture of many. It may also change and morph as you get to know it. When I started shamanic practice, my inner masculine was Christ and then one day it suddenly morphed into Aragorn from Lord of the Rings – which was a nice surprise! Then it settled into a sage, wizard-like being – not one from any tradition, story, or myth – its own form. So, anything can be experienced.

To help you discern I'd encourage you to set aside time on your own. It may be an ongoing exercise which takes several hours and days. Try and be in a room undisturbed, where you are warm and comfortable. Light a candle and set the intention to get to know your allies and archetypical support team. It's nice to play some music such as mantra to support the brain waves to relax. It's also a good idea to breathe and ask the question for each archetype in turn to show themselves and close your eyes for a few minutes of pause before you start to write or draw.

Here are some questions to ask yourself about each archetype:

What is your name?

How old are you?

Where are you from?

What is your role and job?

What is your favourite colour?

What topics will you guide me on?

Where do you live in my body?

Which other archetypes do you relate to?

What is your guidance for me today?

Where on my wheel do you live?

How do I connect with you going forward?

How often would you like me to relate with you?

Do you have the support of a power animal, if so, which one?

What key skill and quality do you gift me?

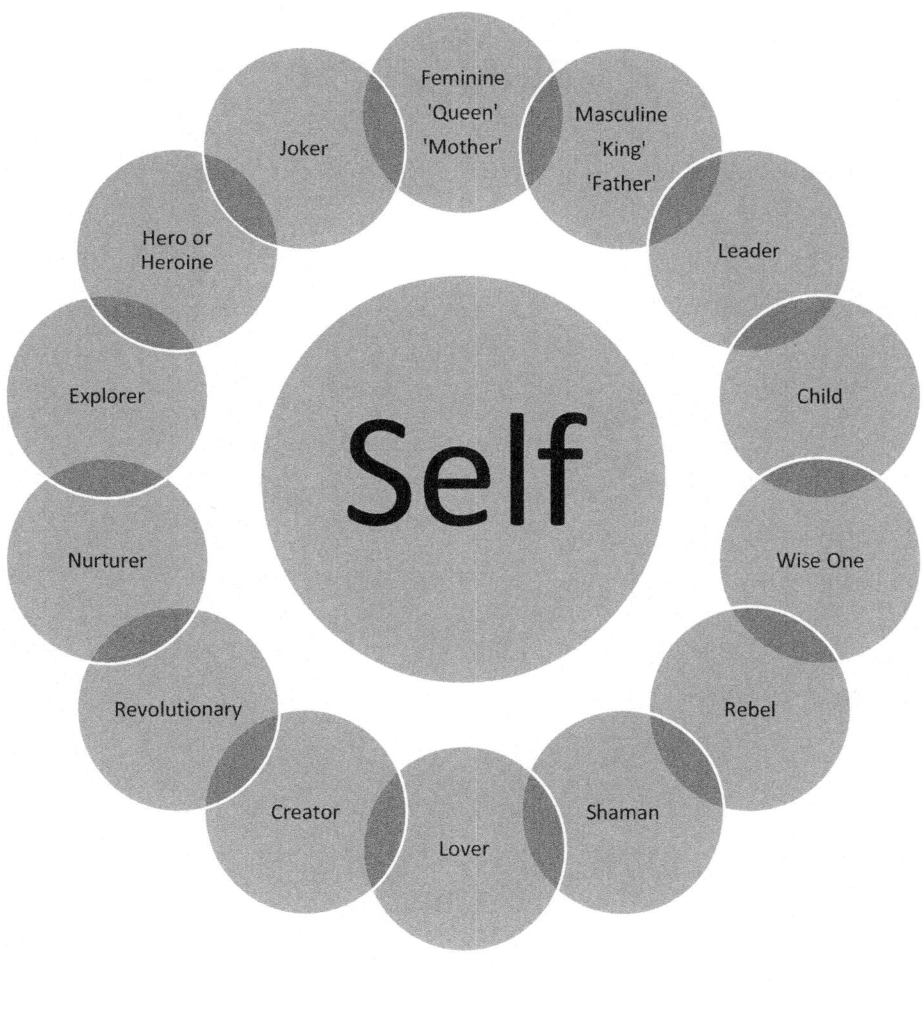

Feminine / 'Queen' / 'Mother'

What is your name?

How old are you?

Where are you from?

What is your role and job?

What is your favourite colour?

What topics will you guide me on?

Where do you live in my body?

Which other archetypes do you relate to?

What is your guidance for me today?

Where on my wheel do you live?

How do I connect with you going forward?

How often would you like me to relate with you?

Do you have the support of a power animal, if so, which one?

What key skill and quality do you gift me?

Masculine / 'King' / 'Father'

What is your name?

How old are you?

Where are you from?

What is your role and job?

What is your favourite colour?

What topics will you guide me on?

Where do you live in my body?

Which other archetypes do you relate to?

What is your guidance for me today?

Where on my wheel do you live?

How do I connect with you going forward?

How often would you like me to relate with you?

Do you have the support of a power animal, if so, which one?

What key skill and quality do you gift me?

Leader

What is your name?

How old are you?

Where are you from?

What is your role and job?

What is your favourite colour?

What topics will you guide me on?

Where do you live in my body?

Which other archetypes do you relate to?

What is your guidance for me today?

Where on my wheel do you live?

How do I connect with you going forward?

How often would you like me to relate with you?

Do you have the support of a power animal, if so, which one?

What key skill and quality do you gift me?

Child

What is your name?

How old are you?

Where are you from?

What is your role and job?

What is your favourite colour?

What topics will you guide me on?

Where do you live in my body?

Which other archetypes do you relate to?

What is your guidance for me today?

Where on my wheel do you live?

How do I connect with you going forward?

How often would you like me to relate with you?

Do you have the support of a power animal, if so, which one?

What key skill and quality do you gift me?

Wise One

What is your name?

How old are you?

Where are you from?

What is your role and job?

What is your favourite colour?

What topics will you guide me on?

Where do you live in my body?

Which other archetypes do you relate to?

What is your guidance for me today?

Where on my wheel do you live?

How do I connect with you going forward?

How often would you like me to relate with you?

Do you have the support of a power animal, if so, which one?

What key skill and quality do you gift me?

Rebel

What is your name?

How old are you?

Where are you from?

What is your role and job?

What is your favourite colour?

What topics will you guide me on?

Where do you live in my body?

Which other archetypes do you relate to?

What is your guidance for me today?

Where on my wheel do you live?

How do I connect with you going forward?

How often would you like me to relate with you?

Do you have the support of a power animal, if so, which one?

What key skill and quality do you gift me?

Shaman

What is your name?

How old are you?

Where are you from?

What is your role and job?

What is your favourite colour?

What topics will you guide me on?

Where do you live in my body?

Which other archetypes do you relate to?

What is your guidance for me today?

Where on my wheel do you live?

How do I connect with you going forward?

How often would you like me to relate with you?

Do you have the support of a power animal, if so, which one?

What key skill and quality do you gift me?

Lover

What is your name?

How old are you?

Where are you from?

What is your role and job?

What is your favourite colour?

What topics will you guide me on?

Where do you live in my body?

Which other archetypes do you relate to?

What is your guidance for me today?

Where on my wheel do you live?

How do I connect with you going forward?

How often would you like me to relate with you?

Do you have the support of a power animal, if so, which one?

What key skill and quality do you gift me?

Creator

What is your name?

How old are you?

Where are you from?

What is your role and job?

What is your favourite colour?

What topics will you guide me on?

Where do you live in my body?

Which other archetypes do you relate to?

What is your guidance for me today?

Where on my wheel do you live?

How do I connect with you going forward?

How often would you like me to relate with you?

Do you have the support of a power animal, if so, which one?

What key skill and quality do you gift me?

Revolutionary

What is your name?

How old are you?

Where are you from?

What is your role and job?

What is your favourite colour?

What topics will you guide me on?

Where do you live in my body?

Which other archetypes do you relate to?

What is your guidance for me today?

Where on my wheel do you live?

How do I connect with you going forward?

How often would you like me to relate with you?

Do you have the support of a power animal, if so, which one?

What key skill and quality do you gift me?

Nurturer

What is your name?

How old are you?

Where are you from?

What is your role and job?

What is your favourite colour?

What topics will you guide me on?

Where do you live in my body?

Which other archetypes do you relate to?

What is your guidance for me today?

Where on my wheel do you live?

How do I connect with you going forward?

How often would you like me to relate with you?

Do you have the support of a power animal, if so, which one?

What key skill and quality do you gift me?

Explorer

What is your name?

How old are you?

Where are you from?

What is your role and job?

What is your favourite colour?

What topics will you guide me on?

Where do you live in my body?

Which other archetypes do you relate to?

What is your guidance for me today?

Where on my wheel do you live?

How do I connect with you going forward?

How often would you like me to relate with you?

Do you have the support of a power animal, if so, which one?

What key skill and quality do you gift me?

Hero or Heroine

What is your name?

How old are you?

Where are you from?

What is your role and job?

What is your favourite colour?

What topics will you guide me on?

Where do you live in my body?

Which other archetypes do you relate to?

What is your guidance for me today?

Where on my wheel do you live?

How do I connect with you going forward?

How often would you like me to relate with you?

Do you have the support of a power animal, if so, which one?

What key skill and quality do you gift me?

Joker

What is your name?

How old are you?

Where are you from?

What is your role and job?

What is your favourite colour?

What topics will you guide me on?

Where do you live in my body?

Which other archetypes do you relate to?

What is your guidance for me today?

Where on my wheel do you live?

How do I connect with you going forward?

How often would you like me to relate with you?

Do you have the support of a power animal, if so, which one?

What key skill and quality do you gift me?

Self

What is your name?

How old are you?

Where are you from?

What is your role and job?

What is your favourite colour?

What topics will you guide me on?

Where do you live in my body?

Which other archetypes do you relate to?

What is your guidance for me today?

Where on my wheel do you live?

How do I connect with you going forward?

How often would you like me to relate with you?

Do you have the support of a power animal, if so, which one?

What key skill and quality do you gift me?

***Try This:* Discerning your Power Animals**

Power animals, as I said earlier, are helpers and support us to energetically shapeshift to harness their energy. They often accompany archetypes and are gatekeepers to parts and the organs of our body.

Here are some examples:

- Owl can support our eyes – so that we can see in the metaphorical 'dark' and from all directions and perspectives.
- Deer allows us to walk lightly through life.
- Salmon helps us navigate magical paths, swim upstream, to move even when going is tough.
- Crow supports us to be vocal, express and navigate change.
- Eagle helps us step out of drama and see the bigger picture.
- Horse gifts us strength and will power.
- Bear is defence and physical strength – helps us become unmovable.
- Cow is a symbol of plenty.

The list is endless, and you will already have an instinct of which animals you need the support of.

The task you are going to do now is to discern the power animal spirit keepers of areas and organs of your body. It is a simple procedure and **all you need is a quiet space, pen and paper**. However, it is useful to light a candle and play some mantra music to support your logical mind to relax during the activity.

You can do this all-in-one go or do it in stages. Each time you come to the discernment process and undertake the task of connecting. **Pause, light a candle and state your intention clearly – 'my intention is to commune with the power animal spirit keeper of my …. X …. (Whichever part of the body you are wanting to connect to)'. Then, if you can, place your hands on the part of the body and list – receive, know, hear, feel, see which animal comes.** It will be instantaneous, quick.

Once the animal is there, ask…

Why it is the power animal of that part of your body?

What is its colour?

Does it have a name?

How old is it?

What is the medicine or gift it is offering that part of your body and why?

How are you to use that power going forward?

Then ask the animal what you need to know about that part of your body.

Finally ask – *which part of my wheel do you inhabit and why?*

Write the name of the animal down and any description or guidance you received. You can return and conjoin to the power animal at any point and ask for direct access to your fleshy knowing and gain answers to questions about your body. I've asked the power animal to show and tell me why I have pain in parts of my body plus which foods were causing my stomach to be upset!

Here are some ideas for areas of your body you can ask to receive the power animal spirit keeper for:

Adrenal Glands

Anus

Back

Brain

Ears

Elbows

Eyes

Feet

Genitals

Hands

Head

Heart

Intestines

Jaw

Kidney

Knees

Legs

Liver

Lungs

Neck

Nose

Shoulders

Spinal Cord

Stomach

Vocal Cords

Womb

Wrists

Remember to write down as much detail as you can about the power animal or spirit keeper and draw it if you can. Alternatively – if there is an area of the body you feel holds a lot of wisdom or you want further fleshy knowing from, once you identify the power animal spirit keeper of it, it's nice to find a picture and print it out to remind you of the shapeshifting ability and skills you have within you. I sometimes have the animal as my phone and laptop screen saver and a picture stuck on the fridge. I keep connected to the power animal receiving its power and guidance during times of transition or difficulty.

Remember that in shapeshifting and inhabiting the animal - growing, slithering, chirping, spreading outstretched wings – you are activating the genes you share with the animal. Have fun!

Try This: **Connecting to the Central Archetype and Power Animal Serpent**

Try this only if you are not phobic of snakes and serpents. If you are, skip it!

As has been discussed, Serpent is the central archetype and animal of the wheel – ouroboros around the rim, core serpent in the centre (running up your nervous system) and then, for me, I have a form of serpent in each part of the wheel.

Serpent is the archetype of regeneration, shedding life, of death, rebirth, life, death, rebirth. It is the archetype of lifeforce, the energy of sacred embodiment and the catalyst of your fleshy knowing. Serpent is a change maker and liberator and for me the ultimate feminist activist, who undoes religion indoctrination and untruth and reinstates within us our sacred bodily appetite, pleasure and desire.

Getting to know your serpent means you get to know your nervous system and lifeforce. It is a somatic experience and embodied shamanic journey. Shapeshifting is part of all cultures, beyond myth, and is an embodied felt sense of the animal self and body. We enter it in flow states easily – we become one with the water when swimming, one with the trees when walking mindfully through the forest. Shapeshifting happens in altered states of consciousness when the logical mind stands down and our senses and faculties become enhanced and amplified. This is often why shamans blind fold themselves during journeys.

To shapeshift and ally with power animals, serpent especially, happens when we return fully to the body and have a direct, experiential knowing – fully received from felt sense, not thoughts. Shapeshifting is visceral. Shapeshifting happens easily and often in dance, sport or theatre – where we take on the mask of another – enact though the body.

To make this connection with serpent (and her different forms if you choose to do so) it will be useful to have a **track of music which is drumming or rattling or a track of music which reminds you of snake movement**. The key, as described earlier in the book in The Tree of Life section, is to **mimic the shape and movement of that which you want to commune more deeply to the energy of**. So, whilst we are doing this for serpent now, you can do it for trees, the sun, insets, the sea, rivers, rocks, the soil, any other animal. In effect it's all of these things are in our cells, as all of the world and universe are connected in chemical compound make up. So, the shape and energy of that which we are wanting to unite with is already within us, waiting to be activated. You can find a link for a toolbox at the end of this book with recommended tracks and other resources.

So *set the intention to move like and as serpent – to learn from her.* Put on the music and allow your body to connect and experience all or any of the following:

- The ouroboros – circular process – shedding, dying, rebirthing – the movement of the wheel
- The nervous system spine life force serpent – the fire rising inside
- The dragon serpent – and her fire breath of winter
- The flying serpent – and her creative ideas and lightness of spring
- The royal cobra – and her full embodiment and pride of summer
- The water serpent – her cooling flow of autumn

Listen through tracking your body. The key is to follow and receive fleshy knowing as serpent.

***Try This:* Discerning the Landscape, Energetic Structure and Gatekeeper of your Under World, Middle World and Upper World**

This final exercise is a creative one and involves you getting to know the landscape, energy and gate keeper of the three worlds within and as your body:

- Upper World – cosmos/heaven/above – branches of the tree – your neck, head and mind, plus stretched arms
- Middle World – earth/consciousness – tree trunk – your torso

- Underworld – unconscious/otherworld/spirit realm – tree roots – your legs and feet

Each world has a spirit keeper, a specific landscape and energetic allies within it such as fire or air deities, spirit beings, etc.

You need to prepare in advance for this. ***You need 3 large pieces of paper, pens, scissors, glue, and lots of old magazines.***

You are going to communicate with the gatekeeper of each world and then **produce a collage** of the world.

You'll need **at least 1 hour for each world**.

Be in a warm room where you won't be interrupted. Put on a piece of music which, for you, represents the world you are connecting to. Light a candle ….

For each world, follow these steps:

> First, call on the gatekeeper of the world and see, feel and know who comes. Once the gatekeeper is there, ask it *why it is the gatekeeper of that world? What is its colour? Does it have a name? How old is it? Finally ask – which part of my wheel do you inhabit and why? What is its primary job?*
>
> Then ask what you need to know about the world.
>
> Then ask for permission to explore the world.
>
> Then create a collage – without thinking – ripping out pictures and gluing or drawing that world – do it without overthinking – just allow it to form – trust how and what unfolds – be drawn to shapes, colours, words. What is the structure?
>
> Thank the gatekeeper and leave the world at the end of the process.

Repeat for each world.

Spend time reflecting on each collage, its messages and meaning.

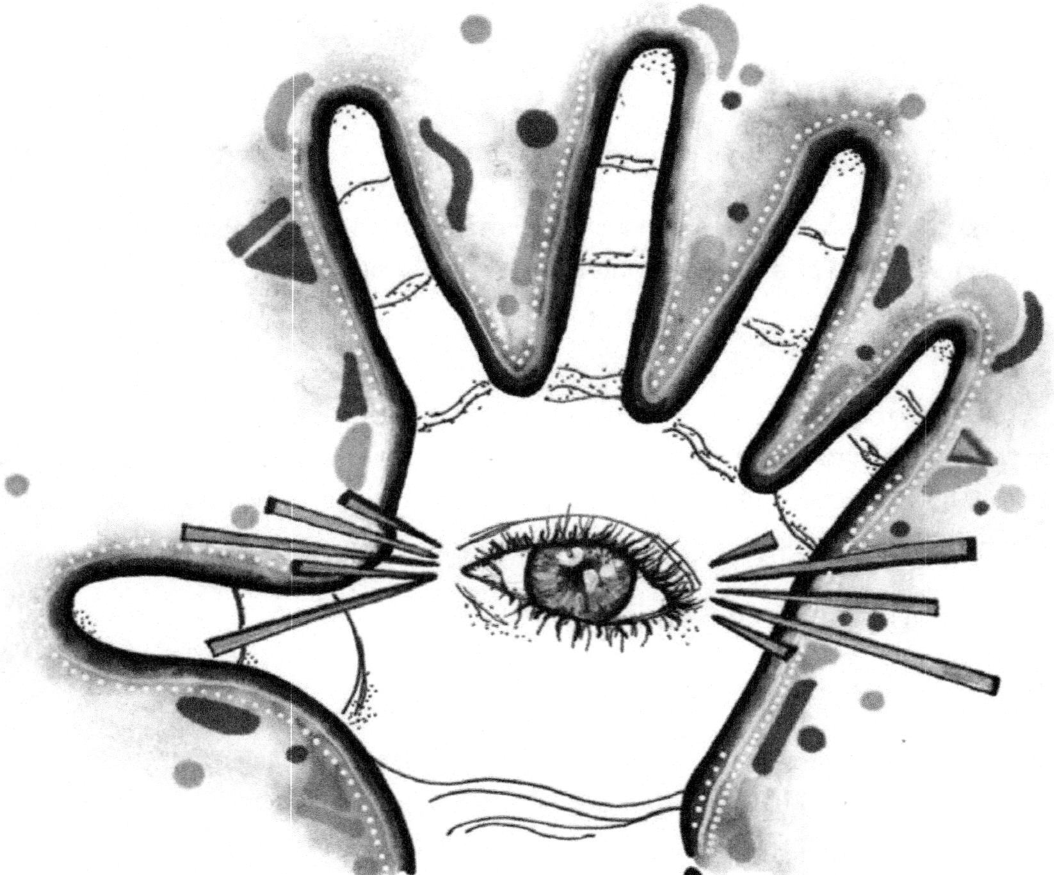

Art by Sophie Skinner

Chapter 4: Accessing your Fleshy Knowing

"Before you can hear, much less follow, the voice of your soul, you have to win back your body. You have to go on a pilgrimage beneath the skin."
– *Meggan Watterson, Reveal*

Your flesh, your animal body, connects you not only to your own 'knowing' but also to the wisdom of your forebears and also all things in the cosmos. Trees, rocks, the soil are all our ancestors – from way back in time. We share cells with all living things, our microbiome swarms with bacteria which operate as a community and link to other microorganism communities – those of insects, fungi. Every living thing shares the fundamental building block of life – carbon (I'd recommend looking at a picture of carbon to see what living things are made of, including you) – and so carbon within us contains ancestry and wisdom. The body we are in right now is a culmination of all times, things and events of what has gone before and through our fleshy knowing we access knowing of all – of everything.

This knowing is not rational, logical or accessed cognitively. We learn through looking out into the world, observing and then becoming that which we observe. To learn the wisdom of the wolf we observe the wolf. Then feel within our bodies the wolf's movement, thoughts, actions, and in becoming it receive wolf's power and wisdom. Our animal body links to theirs.

Feeling into our Self – that part of us beyond thought – the felt sense – we connect, listen and track the movement of our ancestors within us, connecting to their wisdom and sometimes resolving their pain. Gnosis – spiritual internal knowledge – is a felt experience and the realm of the shaman and the mystic. To know something, we become it. Those who can join the dots, psychically and somatically, through shapeshifting – they are the 'seers' and 'shamans'.

The blood in our bodies connects us to the bloodline of our hereditary knowledge – information passed down family blood lines. It contains the wisdom and intelligence of our ancestral lineage, and it is stored somatically. Those who tap into this become the elders and shamanic 'wisdom keepers' of their family lines.

We can look at blood from a micro and a macro perspective. When zooming in we can connect to our own lifespan and the innate intelligence of self – that unique DNA sequence bespoke to us – and the personal wisdom and guidance it offers for our life journey. When zooming out we see the water, salts and proteins in the blood which connect us to the intelligence of all other things – the history, lineage and wisdom which also contain them – the sea, the plants, the sand – much of which is non-human. Through this we become the wisdom keeper of aspects of the universe and the earth.

In connecting at a cellular and physiological level with the earth – in recognising that our body and the body of the earth are inseparable, synced and one in the same, we commune ever more deeply with the wisdom of the land. This is especially potent when connecting with the land we currently live on or were born on. The land has a spirit keeper and through placing your hands on the earth and feeling the pulse of the land – its quality, colour, sensation – we can receive wisdom through and from it.

Within our five senses there is another realm – the extraordinary within the ordinary – the sacred within the mundane – the spirit within the flesh. They coexist. They can be accessed simultaneously. We experience within us, the mystical, shamanic, timelessness, past, present, future of our DNA lines simultaneously – the voices of ancestors – which we both liberate and learn from in hearing them. Within us is a wealth of abundant wisdom.

How do we practise Somatic Shamanism and connect with our somatic intelligence and wisdom?

In some of the earlier *'Try This'* exercises you were introduced to how to begin to facilitate shamanic seeing and knowing. The key to connecting to and accessing fleshy knowing is to set a clear intention and to alter consciousness in a safe and trauma-informed way, so that you do not go up and out (dissociate) but instead go into and through the body and as the Tree of Life.

Accessing the otherworldly, liminal (in between) and alternative, states of consciousness, a fully *embodied* trance state can be done via you choosing the best and safest method which works for you to connect to the 'unseen.' Trance state can feel like a frightening concept but what it means is a soft day-dreamy state. The optimum time for being in a liminal state is 20 minutes at a time, but it is best for you to feel into it. For example, when truly shapeshifting and having a felt sense of some animals – feeling the slither, grind or growl – might be overwhelming for your nervous system, so a minute may be enough. Less is more.

Liminal realms and altered states of consciousness can be evoked safely through activities such as:

- Sound – drumming, rattles, bowls, chimes, singing, chanting, plucking a string
- An audio recording of the above
- Movement – running, swaying, hula hooping, skipping or repetitive dance
- Trance walking in nature
- Communing with the elements – the sea, wind, sun
- Breathing rhythmically
- Sitting on earth and grounding – connecting to the earth's energy field and rooting

- Swimming
- Gazing into a fire or candle

There are other ways, so it is worth doing more research. Trust yourself if you already have a method which supports you to feel in the flow, fluid and connected. You can access a link for a toolbox filled with resources at the end of this book.

Having an intention, what to receive guidance on, whether that be personal or collective, is essential. Shamanic practice is not done to you – you opt in and set clear intent. Asking questions to elicit a clear yes or no answer or setting 'close' intentions are not helpful. Fleshy knowing is not dictatorial but rather suggestive and allows the conscious mind space to process and get on board and interpret the guidance and options offered. So, when forming an intention, keep it open. As yourself, what is it you want guidance about? Then keep repeating the intention – in your mind and out loud during the practice – 'my intention of the journey is ...'

When undertaking a Somatic Shamanic Journey ensure you will be uninterrupted. Choose a safe, quiet and uncluttered space – a clear space. This can be inside or out. Call in the aspects of your wheel – the four directions and elements, above, below, within, without, earth and cosmos and any animals and allies you would like to support you.

You can journey moving or lying down. Follow a journey which unfolds in your mind's eye or in a felt sense way, as sensation, and ensure you move the journey through your body. You begin by imagining or actually enacting walking through a forest, to a fire, to a tree which you hug or touch. The key moment of a Somatic Shamanic Journey is when you become the tree – The Tree of Life – you shapeshift and embody it. Spend a few minutes grounding the feet steadily – rooting as the tree you have become and feel the thickness of the trunk at the base of torso.

All of this will take practise and requires a letting go of control and doubt. Your body will lead you. Then take your hand to the part of the body you're journeying into and through and ask for guidance. Keep repeating the intention, calling on animals, guides and spirit keepers. At the end of the journey say thank you – to your body, mind, heart – to power animals, guides and spirit keepers – to the Tree of Life, above and below.

Remember, you can also creatively journey by free flow creative action – art, sculpture, collage, writing, movement, acting.

A word of caution! The liminal realm and dimension of our flesh is metaphorical, mythic, symbolic, dreamy, fragmentated and coded, but can be very direct and clear at times. It is essential to employ common sense to what you see, feel and know. The logical conscious mind interprets and assesses. Application of critical thinking and combining metacognition, intuition and instinct – is how fleshy knowing can be checked out. Shamanic knowledge is just one aspect of decision-making. As Jung said, 'until you make the unconscious conscious, it will direct your life and you will call it fate.' However, we have many filters and pathways of knowing and all need to be consulted to access wisdom – intuition and cognition – physical and emotional feelings, ancestral patterning, soul messages, and spirit guides are examples.

During shamanic journeys, our allies and guides clarify, protect and support. They also offer healing. Power animals moving in and through the organs of our body can fortify us – needs being met by the spirit of animal or being a support to the body.

We can creatively imagine and use movement to shapeshift and receive support from animals and our allies for our body. Instructing serpent to move through the intestines and help us shed old stuff can relieve constipation. Connecting to the water within the womb and asking for waves of cramping to rise and fall, can help relieve menstrual cramps.

Wisdom involves embodied senses, accessing the senses and evoking embodied trance states to open access to animal body and senses. This needs to be done in a nervous system friendly, regulated and trauma-informed way and that is why it is essential to shapeshift into the Tree of Life first. To ground the feet steadily – root as the tree you are – and feel the thickness of the trunk at the base of torso.

At some times in our lives *Somatic Shamanism* is easier to access – during sudden change, rites of passage or physical change, e.g., first period, childbirth or menopause. Also, monthly during our menstrual bleed, shapeshifting and the liminal day-dreamy imaginal realms and journeys are easier to access more intensely.

At certain times of the year, it is easier to journey into certain parts of the body. Mind, visions and dreams are predominant in winter when we are still, womb and genitals are active at spring supporting us to journey into what is new and next for us, the power of the belly and heart are predominant at summer as we are action-oriented and focused on completing projects – and finally, the intestines are active at autumn, as we give gratitude, harvest, complete and let go.

Drawing imaginatively on traditional stories, folklore, symbology and mythology associated with certain times of the year can be helpful and support us to access fleshy knowing in these areas of the body at those times of year. Here are some of the journeys I have experienced based on my own life experience, learning and culture, at two particular seasons of the year. You can try them out yourself or use them as templates to create your own day-dreamy stories and draw on myths and symbols you associate with the seasons and feel them within to see and know your own fleshy wisdom.

My Spring Somatic Shamanism Journey

At spring I imagine journeying to a dragon egg, in the centre of earth. I bring the egg into my womb space and crack it open using the fire of the mother dragon at the centre of the earth. I feel her blowing her fire between my legs and up through my vagina and anus into my pelvis. The fire in early spring is gentle and warming, it doesn't burn. I bring the fire through the body to my womb where it lights a flame and cracks open the egg, so I have my own internal dragon. I ask that dragon to blow its fire upwards to my heart and light a flame there and then to my mind to light a flame there. The three flames of eros, or passion, from earth now warm me up and bring me back to life after the winter. The element of air at spring innocently fans these flames so the lover energy, fire, can become stronger, ready for summer.

My Summer Somatic Shamanism Journey

I imagine earth's serpent moving up my legs and entering the base of my torso. I put on some music and dance – feeling the serpent move through my body. Then at peak summer I activate the serpent blade of truth, of spirit, within me – to check that what I am creating and doing is aligned. I move my head and shape shift into hooded cobra. I wait from serpent to move through me, until she becomes erect, that a blade of truth – glistening and glinting – running through the central energy of channel of my torso. Poised, I create balance – gently rocking front and back, left and right and feeling the bottom of my torso, my feet and the top of my head, my crown – above and below. When I am absolutely balanced, I check in and ask my mind, body and heart for any guidance of where I need to let go, adjust or amend to maintain this equilibrium and complete projects. That which is not aligned becomes clear – a name, place, image, memory, colour or sensation gifts me the wisdom.

What fleshy knowing might you access?

You may access somatic memories of events you had forgotten in this lifetime, or wisdom within the tissues, muscles and organs of the body. Through witnessing your body so intently and intimately you might release and resolve symptoms you have been experiencing. You might also sense ancestral somatic memory, some of which might be challenging, such as flogging, burning, assault and punishment.

Emotional patterns and genetic behavioural imprints passed down through generations might also be accessed in and through the body e.g., abandonment, addition, scarcity. These somatic imprints hold a charge of energy – and to complete trauma discharge is to release the lifeforce and power of your ancestral lineage.

You may find that you begin to remove density and blocks within your body. As you journey into body parts and organs you might feel there are objects or shapes held there. This is blocked energy or stagnation. In witnessing these and holding your hand to them – seeing and hearing and feeling their messages – they will soften and be transformed into flow. I have experienced blocks of ice, arrows of fire, black squares within parts of my body – all of which held messages and once received, allowed these objects to transform into flowing lifeforce.

You might also find that accessing your fleshy knowing organically supports soul retrieval to happen. Soul retrieval is a shamanic technique of bringing back into the body parts of the soul, your lifeforce and energy which have been in the safe keeping of the earth and other realms. Soul loss happens in times of stress, shock, and trauma. Sensitive aspects of self and soul leave the body in search of a safe space, but the body needs these parts back to feel integrated. When parts of soul and lifeforce returns we may feel tingling, may shake, feel hot and cold. Holding the body through these sensations in a soothing and reassuring way is important.

Soul retrieval might happen once the body gives us a message about something which happened to us or our ancestors which needs to be witnessed. As we see, feel and know in and through the body and the soul part returns we may notice that the soul retrieval is accompanied by a metaphor, gift or being. Soul parts can come back as archetypes – e.g., a jester or a witch or sometimes come back as spiritual beings – an angel or a human role – e.g., CEO, judge, teacher. Trust whatever you see, feel and know – and always ask the body part or organ *why has this soul part been retrieved? What gifts does it offer me? How can I integrate it into my life practically?*

***Try This:* Journey to receive Wisdom from Body Parts and Organs**

Follow the steps below.

1. Breathe in and become the tree – breathe out and settle into connection with the body part or organ.

2. Place your hand on the area of the body where the part or organ is located.

3. Visualise the organ or body part. Sometimes it is a good idea to research where the organ is located and what it looks like in advance.

4. Imagine the palm of your hand has a magic all-seeing eye in the centre, which can look through skin, blood, tissue, bone and so is able to gaze directly at and clearly see the body part or organ.

5. Ask the body part or organ:

   – *Who or what is the gatekeeper of it and why?*

   – *Which power animal is connected to it and why?*

If you have connected to this part or organ before it may be the same animal or it may have changed – trust what you see, feel and know.

What does the part or organ want you to know and why?

Plus, you can ask specific questions to parts and organs. There are some suggestions in the table that follows.

Remember, answers might come as a shape, sensation, story, memory, image, sound or knowing.

Adrenal Glands	*Where and with who do you have to defend yourself and fight?* *Where, from what or who do you want to run away and why?* *Where, doing what and with who do you feel safe?*
Anus	*What blocks you and why?*
Arms	*Where can you reach even higher in your life?* *What can you embrace more of?*
Back	*What or who supports you?*
Bladder	*Who or what really pisses you off?*
Blood	*Where, doing what and with who do you feel alive?*
Bones	*What protects you?* *Where do you feel are the supportive structures in your life?* *What shakes your foundations and why?*
Brain	*Which of your thoughts are unhelpful to you and why?*
Breasts	*What truly nurtures you and why?*
Ears	*What do you need to stop listening to and why?*
Elbows	*Where, what and whom do you need to push away?*
Eyes	*Where do you see beauty in your life and why?*
Feet	*What is your next step?* *Where are you going next?*

Fingers	*What is too fiddly in your life?* *What and from who can you take back?* *What are you grasping too tightly?*
Gallbladder	*What blocks your feelings of worthiness and why?*
Genitals	*What is it you want to create?*
Hands	*What can you hand over to someone else?*
Heart	*What do you need to receive?* *How can you give yourself more compassion?* *What is the greatest love of your life?*
Hips	*What prevents you from moving freely?* *What and with who is life a dance?*
Intestines	*What do you need to let go of and why?*
Jaw	*Where and at whom do you need to growl and why?*
Kidneys	*What, where or with who do you shrivel up or feel sucked dry and why?*
Knees	*Where can you feel yourself giving in and why?* *What causes you to doubt and buckle in life and why?*
Legs	*What brings a spring to your step?* *Where do you feel free and why?*
Liver	*Who, what or where in your life is toxic?*
Lungs	*What takes your breath away?* *Where and why was the wind knocked out of your sails?* *Where and with whom do you 'breathe easy'?*
Mouth	*What are you consuming which isn't working for you?*
Muscles	*When, doing what and with who do you feel helpless and why?* *Where and with who do you need more strength?*
Neck	*What in your life is a pain in the neck and why?*
Nose	*What stinks in your life and why?* *What is past its sell-by date in your life?*
Pelvis	*What turns you on?*

Rib-cage	*Where and with whom do you need to maintain strong boundaries and why?*
Shoulders	*Which responsibility are you carrying which isn't yours to carry and how can you give it back?* *What can you now shrug off?*
Skin	*Where do you need stronger boundaries and why is that?*
Spine	*Where can you go with the flow more?*
Spleen	*What brings you joy and energy?*
Stomach	*What, where and who sickens you?* *What where and who can't you digest and why?*
Teeth	*What does your inner child need from you to feel nourished and cared for?*
Throat	*What's hard for you to swallow in your life and why?*
Thyroid	*What is your truth?*
Tongue	*What in your life leaves a bitter taste in your mouth?*
Voice Box (Larynx)	*Which words need to be said and to whom?*
Womb	*Who or what do you desire?*
Wrists	*What is too heavy to hold in your life?* *What weighs you down?*

Through *Somatic Shamanism* your fleshy knowing communicates in sounds, colours, shapes. Wisdom which comes in and through the body is about connecting to sensation and emotional literacy. Descriptions and wisdom are rarely given through words, but you can ask the sensation why it is there? Or, ask the body part or organ if it could speak, *what would it say?* Or, *how old is it?* Or, *who is the gatekeeper of the organ and why?*

Give each body part the attention it deserves on the pages that follow. Follow the steps below.

1. Breathe in and become the tree – breathe out and settle into connection with the body part or organ.

2. Place your hand on the area of the body where the part or organ is located.

3. Visualise the organ or body part. Sometimes it is a good idea to research where the organ is located and what it looks like in advance.
4. Imagine the palm of your hand has a magic all-seeing eye in the centre, which can look through skin, blood, tissue, bone and so is able to gaze directly at and clearly see the body part or organ.
5. Ask the body part or organ: *Who or what is the gatekeeper of it and why? Which power animal is connected to it and why?*

It can be helpful to have a journal and note down what you see, feel and know immediately after completing a journey or practice, as on reflecting on this you can gain more insights. Plus, if you journey into a body part or organ several times you might find the narrative or guidance you receive develops in what you experienced and knew previously.

Adrenal Glands

Where and with who do you have to defend yourself and fight?

Where, from what or who do you want to run away and why?

Where, doing what and with who do you feel safe?

If your adrenal glands could speak, *what would they say?*

How old are they?

Who is the gatekeeper of your adrenal glands and why?

Which power animal is connected to them and why?

Anus

What blocks you and why?

If your anus could speak, *what would it say?*

How old is it?

Who is the gatekeeper of your anus and why?

Which power animal is connected to it and why?

Arms

Where can you reach even higher in your life?

What can you embrace more of?

If your arms could speak, *what would they say?*

How old are they?

Who is the gatekeeper of your arms and why?

Which power animal is connected to them and why?

Back

What or who supports you?

If your back could speak, *what would it say?*

How old is it?

Who is the gatekeeper of your back and why?

Which power animal is connected to it and why?

Bladder

Who or what really pisses you off?

If your bladder could speak, *what would it say?*

How old is it?

W*ho is the gatekeeper of your bladder and why?*

Which power animal is connected to it and why?

Blood

Where, doing what and with who do you feel alive?

If your blood could speak, *what would it say?*

How old is it?

Who is the gatekeeper of your blood and why?

Which power animal is connected to it and why?

Bones

What protects you?

Where do you feel are the supportive structures in your life?

What shakes your foundations and why?

If your bones could speak, *what would they say?*

How old are they?

Who is the gatekeeper of your bones and why?

Which power animal is connected to them and why?

Brain

Which of your thoughts are unhelpful to you and why?

If your brain could speak, *what would it say?*

How old is it?

Who is the gatekeeper of your brain and why?

Which power animal is connected to it and why?

Breasts

What truly nurtures you and why?

If your breasts could speak, *what would they say?*

How old are they?

Who is the gatekeeper of your breasts and why?

Which power animal is connected to them and why?

Ears

What do you need to stop listening to and why?

If your ears could speak, *what would they say?*

How old are they?

Who *is the gatekeeper of your ears and why?*

Which power animal is connected to them and why?

Elbows

Where, what and whom do you need to push away?

If your elbows could speak, *what would they say?*

How old are they?

Who is the gatekeeper of your elbows and why?

Which power animal is connected to them and why?

Eyes

Where do you see beauty in your life and why?

If your eyes could speak, *what would they say?*

How old are they?

Who is the gatekeeper of your eyes and why?

Which power animal is connected to them and why?

Feet

What is your next step?

Where are you going next?

If your feet could speak, *what would they say?*

How old are they?

Who *is the gatekeeper of your feet and why?*

Which power animal is connected to them and why?

Fingers

What is too fiddly in your life?

What and from who can you take back?

What are you grasping too tightly?

If your fingers could speak, *what would they say?*

How old are they?

Who is the gatekeeper of your fingers and why?

Which power animal is connected to them and why?

Gallbladder

What blocks your feelings of worthiness and why?

If your gallbladder could speak, *what would it say?*

How old is it?

Who is the gatekeeper of your gallbladder and why?

Which power animal is connected to it and why?

Genitals

What is it you want to create?

If your genitals could speak, *what would they say?*

How old are they?

Who is the gatekeeper of your genitals and why?

Which power animal is connected to them and why?

Hands

What can you hand over to someone else?

If your hands could speak, *what would they say?*

How old are they?

Who is the gatekeeper of your hands and why?

Which power animal is connected to it and why?

Heart

What do you need to receive?

How can you give yourself more compassion?

What is the greatest love of your life?

If your heart could speak, *what would it say?*

How old is it?

Who *is the gatekeeper of your heart and why?*

Which power animal is connected to it and why?

Hips

What prevents you from moving freely?

What and with who is life a dance?

If your hips could speak, *what would they say?*

How old are they?

Who is the gatekeeper of your hips and why?

Which power animal is connected to them and why?

Intestines

What do you need to let go of and why?

If your intestines could speak, *what would they say?*

How old are they?

Who is the gatekeeper of your intestines and why?

Which power animal is connected to it and why?

Jaw

Where and at whom do you need to growl and why?

If your jaw could speak, *what would it say?*

How old is it?

Who is the gatekeeper of your jaw and why?

Which power animal is connected to it and why?

Kidneys

What, where or with who do you shrivel up or feel sucked dry and why?

If your kidneys could speak, *what would they say?*

How old are they?

Who is the gatekeeper of your kidneys and why?

Which power animal is connected to it and why?

Knees

Where can you feel yourself giving in and why?

What causes you to doubt and buckle in life and why?

If your knees could speak, *what would they say?*

How old are they?

Who is the gatekeeper of your knees and why?

Which power animal is connected to them and why?

Legs

What brings a spring to your step?

Where do you feel free and why?

If your legs could speak, *what would they say?*

How old are they?

Who is the gatekeeper of your legs and why?

Which power animal is connected to it and why?

Liver

Who, what or where in your life is toxic?

If your liver could speak, *what would it say?*

How old is it?

Who is the gatekeeper of your liver and why?

Which power animal is connected to it and why?

Lungs

What takes your breath away?

Where and why was the wind knocked out of your sails?

Where and with whom do you 'breathe easy'?

If your lungs could speak, *what would they say?*

How old are they?

Who is the gatekeeper of your lungs and why?

Which power animal is connected to them and why?

Mouth

What are you consuming which isn't working for you?

If your mouth could speak, *what would it say?*

How old is it?

Who is the gatekeeper of your mouth and why?

Which power animal is connected to it and why?

Muscles

When, doing what and with who do you feel helpless and why?

Where and with who do you need more strength?

If your muscles could speak, *what would they say?*

How old are they?

Who is the gatekeeper of your muscles and why?

Which power animal is connected to them and why?

Neck

What in your life is a pain in the neck and why?

If your neck could speak, *what would it say?*

How old is it?

Who is the gatekeeper of your neck and why?

Which power animal is connected to it and why?

Nose

What stinks in your life and why?

What is past its sell-by date in your life?

If your nose could speak, *what would it say?*

How old is it?

Who is the gatekeeper of your nose and why?

Which power animal is connected to it and why?

Pelvis

What turns you on?

If your pelvis could speak, *what would it say?*

How old is it?

Who is the gatekeeper of your pelvis and why?

Which power animal is connected to it and why?

Rib Cage

Where and with whom do you need to maintain strong boundaries and why?

If your rib cage could speak, *what would it say?*

How old is it?

Who is the gatekeeper of your rib cage and why?

Which power animal is connected to it and why?

Shoulders

Which responsibility are you carrying which isn't yours to carry and how can you give it back?

What can you now shrug off?

If your shoulders could speak, *what would they say?*

How old are they?

Who is the gatekeeper of your shoulders and why?

Which power animal is connected to them and why?

Skin

Where do you need stronger boundaries and why is that?

If your skin could speak, *what would it say?*

How old is it?

Who is the gatekeeper of your skin and why?

Which power animal is connected to it and why?

Spine

Where can you go with the flow more?

If your spine could speak, *what would it say?*

How old is it?

Who *is the gatekeeper of your spine and why?*

Which power animal is connected to it and why?

Spleen

What brings you joy and energy?

If your spleen could speak, *what would it say?*

How old is it?

Who is the gatekeeper of your spleen and why?

Which power animal is connected to it and why?

Stomach

What, where and who sickens you?

What where and who can't you digest and why?

If your stomach could speak, *what would it say?*

How old is it?

Who is the gatekeeper of your stomach and why?

Which power animal is connected to it and why?

Teeth

What does your inner child need from you to feel nourished and cared for?

If your teeth could speak, *what would they say?*

How old are they?

Who is the gatekeeper of your teeth and why?

Which power animal is connected to them and why?

Throat

What's hard for you to swallow in your life and why?

If your throat could speak, *what would it say?*

How old is it?

Who is the gatekeeper of your throat and why?

Which power animal is connected to it and why?

Thyroid

What is your truth?

If your thyroid could speak, *what would it say?*

How old is it?

Who is the gatekeeper of your thyroid and why?

Which power animal is connected to it and why?

Tongue

What in your life leaves a bitter taste in your mouth?

If your tongue could speak, *what would it say?*

How old is it?

Who is the gatekeeper of your tongue and why?

Which power animal is connected to it and why?

Voice Box (Larynx)

Which words need to be said and to whom?

If your Larynx could speak, *what would it say?*

How old is it?

Who is the gatekeeper of your voice box and why?

Which power animal is connected to it and why?

Womb

Who or what do you desire?

If your womb could speak, *what would it say?*

How old is it?

Who is the gatekeeper of your womb and why?

Which power animal is connected to it and why?

Wrists

What is too heavy to hold in your life?

What weighs you down?

If your wrists could speak, *what would they say?*

How old are they?

Who is the gatekeeper of your wrists and why?

Which power animal is connected to them and why?

***Try This:* Somatic Shamanism at the End of the Day**

This simple tool is a beautiful way of cultivating connecting to your fleshy knowing and going in and through the body. An added bonus is that it is highly regulating for the nervous system too. When in bed and getting ready for sleep, place your hand on your forehead and ask for guidance on an issue from the day.

If you notice any tension or discomfort in the body, place your hand over the area and breathe into the area – exhaling and offering presence and the invitation for release. Then ask your body for guidance. What does the tension or discomfort want you to know?

***Try This:* Somatic Shamanism and the Earth**

Deepening into your *Somatic Shamanism* path and the guidance you receive through your senses, goes hand in hand with deepening your connection with the Earth *and* the point of connection of your body and the Earth. Paying close attention to the area of your body that touches the earth, or where your skin – and the water, rain, river or the sea meets, where the heat of the sun warms your face, arms or legs – or the sensation of the wind on your face – this area of union holds personal and universal fleshy knowing.

You are yourself – but also your descendants and future generations, all things past, present and future – one with the Earth and elements. In deepening into the union, you expand the wisdom on Self and retrieve the wisdom of your ancestral lines.

Two conscious practices to facilitate this deepening relationship are below.

Practice 1.

Hold the soil or a shell, stone or rock from the land on which you find yourself. This can be the area on which you live, the land of your forebears or somewhere you are visiting. In feeling the elements, you share in common with the object – what both you and the object contain – you connect to the fleshy wisdom of your ancestors who had walked on the land before you – doing the same and receiving their wisdom and insights.

Practice 2.

Offer your DNA to the land on which you live as an offering of gratitude, reciprocity and respect. Hold the intention to create loving union with the land and pledge to reverently preserve and protect it. You can do this by burying some of your hair in the earth, urinating on the land or offering your menstrual blood with sacred intention. Feel how you move with the seasons and weather systems more deeply in doing so. You may find you are able to connect with the wisdom of the land, its gatekeepers and ancestors who lived previously on it alongside being able to commune more somatically with the elements, weather systems and needs of the earth.

Conclusion

Body and spirit – there is no separation. My hope is that this book has supported you to recover fleshy knowing. May you live as the Tree of Life, fully connected to your shamanic self, ancestral wisdom and gnosis.

May you remember that the whole universe is within you, and you are within the whole universe. May you treat the earth and all living beings well for in doing so you are caring for yourself and future generations.

Kay Louise Aldred

Further Exploration

Nervous system: https://irenelyon. com/ and https://kimberlyannjohnson. com/

The Book of Symbols: Reflections on Archetypal Images (The Archive for Research in Archetypal Symbolism)

Toolbox: https://thegirlgod.com/ss_toolkit.php

An online evergreen 'Experience to Share' course.

https://thegirlgod.com/somatic_shamanism_course.php

About the Artists

Kat Shaw is a prolific artist who connects to Goddesses from all over the world.

She works tirelessly to breathe life into these Divine Goddesses, making each painting not only unique and vibrant, but also infusing them to carry and share the particular energy and personality of each Goddess.

Kat is committed to empowering and inspiring people of all ages to grow and reach their full potential.

Through her wellbeing business "Fabulously Imperfect", her artwork, her Reiki and her dedication to Goddess energy, Kat sprinkles her magic around like glitter!

She is specifically dedicated to encouraging women, believing that it is time to rise together – supporting each other and celebrating ourselves as the magnificent Goddesses that we really are.

You can find Kat online at @katshawartist and her website is https://katshaw.art.

I am **Soph Skinner**, a 26-year-old creatrix.

Addicted to diving into the deeper, darker and elevated, angelic parts of my inner being through art and poetry. With all my creative outlets I am constantly transmuting and rebirthing myself to become all that I want to be. I'd love you to join me on this journey and share yours with me!

I specialise in graphic art, bringing your inner visions, dreams and desires to life in the physical realm.

As a poetry writer and lover, words are my main source of inspiration and always have been. This is why I work so closely with sigils. To me a sigil is a form of symbol that holds our intentions- we make an intention in words and by sealing it within a symbol it helps us take action to change our reality and manifest our desires in life. In my own ritual practices, I create an art work with each full and new moon.

You can find Sophie on Instagram at @she_who_creatrix and her website is https://shewhocreatrix.uk.

Thanks

Heartfelt appreciation to **Trista Hendren** for saying yes (again) to this project and her continual grace, enthusiasm, and expert editing, which she effortlessly does alongside her amazing mum, **Pat Daly**, for whom I am also grateful.

A huge thank you to **Kat Shaw** for saying yes to her art being used for the cover of this book – this was a huge honour, and the image, for me, is a perfect depiction of a woman embodying her shamanic self. You can find Kat online at @katshawartist and her website is https://katshaw.art.

Gratitude to **Sophie Skinner** for the beautiful, bespoke images she conjured up from her fabulous imagination in response to my random brief. She's magical. You can find Sophie on Instagram at @she_who_creatrix and her website is https://shewhocreatrix.uk.

A special thanks to **Cissi Williams** who was trained by **The Four Winds** and introduced me to Shamanism and led me through my formative training. Thank you also to all the women I have journeyed with and those I have had the privilege to facilitate for and take on a journey around the shamanic wheel. In teaching I learn.

My deepest gratitude goes to my two greatest teachers –**my own body and the Earth**, from which I have learned reciprocity and the ultimate lessons of respect, reverence and right relationship. As within so without, as without, so within.

Finally, deepest love and gratitude for my husband **Dan**. I could not do this work without his love, support and encouragement.

If you enjoyed this book, please consider writing a
brief review on Amazon and/or Goodreads.

We LOVE photos of our readers with Girl God Books! Tag @girlgodbooks on social media – or email them to support@girlgod.org.

What's Next?

Embodied Education: Creating Safe Space for Learning, Facilitating and Sharing – Kay Louise Aldred and Dan Aldred

Pain Perspectives: Finding Meaning in the Fire – Edited by Kay Louise Aldred, Trista Hendren, and Pat Daly

Wounded Feminine: Grieving with Goddess – Edited by Claire Dorey, Trista Hendren, and Pat Daly

Sacred Breasts: an Inspirational Anthology for Living Your Breast Life – Edited by Barbara O'Meara, Trista Hendren, and Pat Daly

Goddess Chants and Songs Book – Edited by Trista Hendren, Anique Radiant Heart, and Pat Daly

Heart to Heart: Words from Goddess/Divine Feminine Wisdom – Kat Shaw

Imperfectly Fabulous – Kat Shaw

Anthologies and children's books on the Black Madonna, Mary Magdalene, Mother Mary, Cerridwen, Aradia, Kali, Brigid, Sophia, Spider Woman, Persephone, The Old Antlered One/Ancient Deer Goddess, An' Cailleach and Hecate are also in the works. Details to be announced.

http://thegirlgod.com/publishing.php

Printed in Great Britain
by Amazon

27375596R00084